Trans
Liberation

ALSO BY *Leslie Feinberg*

Transgender Warriors

Stone Butch Blues

Leslie Feinberg

Trans Liberation

BEYOND PINK OR BLUE

BEACON PRESS

BOSTON

Beacon Press
25 Beacon Street
Boston, Massachusetts 02108-2892
www.beacon.org

Beacon Press books are published under the auspices
of the Unitarian Universalist Association of Congregations.

09 08 07   11 10 9

Book design and formatting by Lucinda L. Hitchcock

This book is printed on acid-free paper that meets the uncoated paper
ANSI / NISO specifications for permanence as revised in 1992.

LIBRARY OF CONGRESS CATALOGING-IN-PUBLICATION DATA
Feinberg, Leslie, 1949–
Trans liberation : beyond pink or blue / by Leslie Feinberg.
p.   cm.
ISBN 0-8070-7950-2 (cloth) ISBN 0-8070-7951-0 (paper)
1. Transsexualism – United States. 2. Transsexuals – United States.
3. Transvestites – United States. 4. Gender identity – United States.
1. Title.
HQ77.95.U6F45   1998   98-16476
305.9' 066 – dc21

Dedicated with my love to the memory of
revolutionary leader Dorothy "Dotty" Ballan
who urged me to develop
a vocabulary of persuasion

Rise like Lions after slumber
In unvanquishable number —
Shake your chains to earth like dew
Which in sleep had fallen on you —
Ye are many — they are few.

PERCY BYSSHE SHELLEY

Contents

1.

*T*he sight of pink-blue gender-coded infant outfits may grate on your nerves. Or you may be a woman or a man who feels at home in those categories. Trans liberation defends you both.

Each person should have the right to *choose* between pink or blue tinted gender categories, as well as all the other hues of the palette. At this moment in time, that right is denied to us. But together, we could make it a reality.

And that's what this book is all about.

I am a human being who would rather not be addressed as Ms. or Mr., ma'am or sir. I prefer to use gender-neutral pronouns like *sie* (pronounced like "*see*") and *hir* (pronounced like "*here*") to describe myself. I am a person who faces almost insurmountable difficulty when instructed to check off an "F" or an "M" box on identification papers.

I'm not at odds with the fact that I was born female-bodied. Nor do I identify as an intermediate sex. I simply do not fit the prevalent Western concepts of what a woman or a man "should" look like. And that reality has dramatically directed the course of my life.

I'll give you a graphic example. From December 1995 to December 1996, I was dying of endocarditis – a bacterial infection that lodges and proliferates in the valves of the heart. A simple blood culture would have immediately exposed the root cause of my raging fevers. Eight weeks of 'round-the-clock intravenous antibiotic drips would have eradicated every last seedling of bacterium in the canals of my heart. Yet I experienced such hatred from some health practitioners that I very nearly died.

I remember late one night in December my lover and I arrived at a hospital emergency room during a snowstorm. My fever was 104 degrees and rising. My blood pressure was pounding dangerously high. The staff immediately hooked me up to monitors and worked to bring down my fever. The doctor in charge began physically examining me. When he determined that my anatomy was female, he flashed me a mean-spirited smirk. While keeping his eyes fixed on me, he approached one of the nurses, seated at a desk, and began rubbing her neck and shoulders. He talked to her about sex for a few minutes. After his pointed demonstration of "normal sexuality," he told me to get dressed and then he stormed out of the room. Still delirious, I struggled to put on my clothes and make sense of what was happening.

The doctor returned after I was dressed. He ordered me to leave the hospital and never return. I refused. I told him I wouldn't leave until he could tell me why my fever was so high. He said, "You have a fever because you are a very troubled person."

This doctor's prejudices, directed at me during a moment of catastrophic illness, could have killed me. The death certificate would have read: Endocarditis. By all rights it should have read: Bigotry.

As my partner and I sat bundled up in a cold car outside the emergency room, still reverberating from the doctor's hatred, I thought about how many people have been turned away from medical care when they were desperately ill – some because an apartheid "whites only" sign hung over the emergency room entrance, or some because their visible Kaposi's sarcoma lesions kept personnel far from their beds. I remembered how a blemish that wouldn't heal drove my mother to visit her doctor repeatedly during the 1950s. I recalled the doctor finally wrote a prescription for Valium because he decided she was a hysterical woman. When my mother finally got to specialists, they told her the cancer had already reached her brain.

Bigotry exacts its toll in flesh and blood. And left unchecked and unchallenged, prejudices create a poisonous climate for us all. Each of us has a stake in the demand that every human being has a right to a job, to shelter, to health care, to dignity, to respect.

I am very grateful to have this chance to open up a conversation with you about why it is so vital to also defend the right of individuals to express and define their sex and gender, and to control their own bodies. For me, it's a life-and-death question. But I also believe that this discussion will have great meaning for you. All your life you've heard such dogma about what it means to be a "real" woman or a "real" man. And chances are you've choked on some of it. You've balked at the idea that being a woman means having to be thin as a rail, emotionally nurturing, and an airhead when it comes to balancing her checkbook. You know in your guts that being a man has nothing to do with rippling muscles, innate courage, or knowing how to handle a chain saw. These are really caricatures. Yet these images have been drilled into us through popular culture and education over the years. And subtler, equally insidious messages lurk in the interstices of these grosser concepts. These ideas of what a "real" woman or man should be straightjacket the freedom of individual self-expression. These gender messages play on and on in a continuous loop in our brains, like commercials that can't be muted.

But in my lifetime I've also seen social upheavals challenge this sex and gender doctrine. As a child who grew up during the Mc-Carthyite, Father-Knows-Best 1950s, and who came of age during the second wave of women's liberation in the United States, I've seen transformations in the ways people think and talk about what it means to be a woman or a man.

Today the gains of the 1970s women's liberation movement are under siege by right-wing propagandists. But many today who are too young to remember what life was like before the women's movement need to know that this was a tremendously progressive development that won significant economic and social reforms. And this struggle by women and their allies swung human consciousness forward like a pendulum.

The movement replaced the common usage of vulgar and diminutive words to describe females with the word *woman* and infused that word with strength and pride. Women, many of them formerly isolated, were drawn together into consciousness-raising groups. Their discussions – about the root of women's oppression and how to eradicate it – resonated far beyond the rooms in which they took place. The women's liberation movement sparked a mass conversation about the systematic degradation, violence, and discrimination that women faced in this society. And this consciousness raising changed many of the ways women and men thought about themselves and their relation to each other. In retrospect, however, we must not forget that these widespread discussions were not just organized to *talk* about oppression. They were a giant dialogue about how to take action to fight institutionalized anti-woman attitudes, rape and battering, the illegality of abortion, employment and education discrimination, and other ways women were socially and economically devalued.

This was a big step forward for humanity. And even the period of political reaction that followed has not been able to overturn all the gains made by that important social movement.

Now another movement is sweeping onto the stage of history: Trans liberation. We are again raising questions about the societal treatment of people based on their sex and gender expression. This discussion will make new contributions to human consciousness. And trans communities, like the women's movement, are carrying out these mass conversations with the goal of creating a movement capable of fighting for justice – of righting the wrongs.

We are a movement of masculine females and feminine males, cross-dressers, transsexual men and women, intersexuals born on the anatomical sweep between female and male, gender-blenders, many other sex and gender-variant people, and our significant others. All told, we expand understanding of how many ways there are to be a human being.

Our lives are proof that sex and gender are much more complex than a delivery room doctor's glance at genitals can determine, more variegated than pink or blue birth caps. We are oppressed for not fitting those narrow social norms. We are fighting back.

Our struggle will also help expose some of the harmful myths about what it means to be a woman or a man that have compartmentalized and distorted your life, as well as mine. Trans liberation has meaning for you – no matter how you define or express your sex or your gender.

If you are a trans person, you face horrendous social punishments — from institutionalization to gang rape, from beatings to denial of child visitation. This oppression is faced, in varying degrees, by all who march under the banner of trans liberation. This brutalization and degradation strips us of what we could achieve with our individual lifetimes.

And if you do not identify as transgender or transsexual or intersexual, your life is diminished by our oppression as well. Your own choices as a man or a woman are sharply curtailed. Your individual journey to express yourself is shunted into one of two deeply carved ruts, and the social baggage you are handed is already packed.

So the defense of each individual's right to control their own body, and to explore the path of self-expression, enhances your own freedom to discover more about yourself and your potentialities. This movement will give you more room to breathe — to be yourself. To discover on a deeper level what it means to be your self.

Together, I believe we can forge a coalition that can fight on behalf of your oppression as well as mine. Together, we can raise each other's grievances and win the kind of significant change we all long for. But the foundation of unity is understanding. So let me begin by telling you a little bit about myself.

I am a human being who unnerves some people. As they look at me, they see a kaleidoscope of characteristics they associate with both males and females. I appear to be a tangled knot of gender contradictions. So they feverishly press the question on me: woman or man? Those are the only two words most people have as tools to shape their question.

"Which sex are you?" I understand their question. It sounds so simple. And I'd like to offer them a simple resolution. But merely answering woman or man will not bring relief to the questioner. As long as people try to bring me into focus using only those two lenses, I will always appear to be an enigma.

The truth is I'm no mystery. I'm a female who is more masculine than those prominently portrayed in mass culture. Millions of females and millions of males in this country do not fit the cramped compartments of gender that we have been taught are "natural" and "normal." For many of us, the words *woman* or *man*, *ma'am* or *sir*, *she* or *he* – in and of themselves – do not total up the sum of our identities or of our oppressions. Speaking for myself, my life only comes into focus when the word *transgender* is added to the equation.

Simply answering whether I was born female or male will not solve the conundrum. Before I can even begin to respond to the question of my own birth sex, I feel it's important to challenge the assumption that the answer is always as simple as either-or. I believe we need to take a critical look at the assumption that is built into the seemingly innocent question: "What a beautiful baby – is it a boy or a girl?"

The human anatomical spectrum can't be understood, let alone appreciated, as long as female or male are considered to be all that exists. "Is it a boy or a girl?" Those are the only two categories allowed on birth certificates.

But this either-or leaves no room for intersexual people, born between the poles of female and male. Human anatomy continues to burst the confines of the contemporary concept that nature delivers all babies on two unrelated conveyor belts. So are the birth certificates changed to reflect human anatomy? No, the U.S. medical establishment hormonally molds and shapes and surgically hacks away at the exquisite complexities of intersexual infants until they neatly fit one category or the other.

A surgeon decides whether a clitoris is "too large" or a penis is "too small." That's a highly subjective decision for anyone to make about another person's body. Especially when the person making the arbitrary decision is scrubbed up for surgery! And what is the criterion for a penis being "too small"? Too small for successful heterosexual intercourse. Intersexual infants are already being tailored for their sexuality, as well as their sex. The infants have no say over what happens to their bodies. Clearly the struggle against genital mutilation must begin here, within the borders of the United States.

But the question asked of all new parents: "Is it a boy or a girl?" is not such a simple question when transsexuality is taken into account, either. Legions of out-and-proud transsexual men and women demonstrate that individuals have a deep, developed, and valid sense of their own sex that does not always correspond to the cursory decision made by a delivery-room obstetrician. Nor is transsexuality a recent phenomenon. People have undergone social sex reassignment and surgical and hormonal sex changes throughout the breadth of oral and recorded human history.

Having offered this view of the complexities and limitations of birth classification, I have no hesitancy in saying I was born female. But that answer doesn't clear up the confusion that drives some people to ask me "Are you a man or a woman?" The problem is that they are trying to understand my gender expression by determining my sex – and therein lies the rub! Just as most of us grew up with only the concepts of *woman* and *man*, the terms *feminine* and *masculine* are the only two tools most people have to talk about the complexities of gender expression.

That pink-blue dogma assumes that biology steers our social destiny. We have been taught that being born female or male will determine how we will dress and walk, whether we will prefer our hair shortly cropped or long and flowing, whether we will be emotionally nurturing or repressed. According to this way of thinking, masculine females are trying to look "like men," and feminine males are trying to act "like women."

But those of us who transgress those gender assumptions also shatter their inflexibility.

So why do I sometimes describe myself as a masculine female? Isn't each of those concepts very limiting? Yes. But placing the two words together is incendiary, exploding the belief that gender expression is linked to birth sex like horse and carriage. It is the social contradiction missing from Dick-and-Jane textbook education.

I actually chafe at describing myself as masculine. For one thing, masculinity is such an expansive territory, encompassing boundaries of nationality, race, and class. Most importantly, individuals blaze their own trails across this landscape.

And it's hard for me to label the intricate matrix of my gender as simply masculine. To me, branding individual self-expression as simply feminine or masculine is like asking poets: Do you write in English or Spanish? The question leaves out the possibilities that the poetry is woven in Cantonese or Ladino, Swahili or Arabic. The question deals only with the system of language that the poet has been taught. It ignores the words each writer hauls up, hand over hand, from a common well. The music words make when finding themselves next to each other for the first time. The silences echoing in the space between ideas. The powerful winds of passion and belief that move the poet to write.

That is why I do not hold the view that gender is simply a social construct — one of two languages that we learn by rote from early age. To me, gender is the poetry each of us makes out of the language we are taught. When I walk through the anthology of the world, I see individuals express their gender in exquisitely complex and ever-changing ways, despite the laws of pentameter.

So how can gender expression be mandated by edict and enforced by law? Isn't that like trying to handcuff a pool of mercury? It's true that human self-expression is diverse and is often expressed in ambiguous or contradictory ways. And what degree of gender expression is considered "acceptable" can depend on your social situation, your race and nationality, your class, and whether you live in an urban or rural environment.

But no one can deny that rigid gender education begins early on in life — from pink and blue color-coding of infant outfits to gender-labeling toys and games. And those who overstep these arbitrary borders are punished. Severely. When the steel handcuffs tighten, it is human bones that crack. No one knows how many trans lives have been lost to police brutality and street-corner bashing. The lives of trans people are so depreciated in this society that many murders go unreported. And those of us who have survived are deeply scarred by daily run-ins with hate, discrimination, and violence.

Trans people are still literally social outlaws. And that's why I am willing at times, publicly, to reduce the totality of my self-expression to descriptions like masculine female, butch, bulldagger, drag king, cross-dresser. These terms describe outlaw status. And I hold my head up proudly in that police lineup. The word *outlaw* is not hyperbolic. I have been locked up in jail by cops because I was wearing a suit and tie. Was my clothing really a crime? Is it a "man's" suit if I am wearing it? At what point – from field to rack – is fiber assigned a sex?

The reality of why I was arrested was as cold as the cell's cement floor: I am considered a masculine female. That's a *gender* violation. My feminine drag queen sisters were in nearby cells, busted for wearing "women's" clothing. The cells that we were thrown into had the same design of bars and concrete. But when we – gay drag kings and drag queens – were thrown into them, the cops referred to the cells as bull's tanks and queen's tanks. The cells were named after our crimes: gender transgression. Actual statutes against cross-dressing and cross-gendered behavior still exist in written laws today. But even where the laws are not written down, police, judges, and prison guards are empowered to carry out merciless punishment for sex and gender "difference."

I believe we need to sharpen our view of how repression by the police, courts, and prisons, as well as all forms of racism and bigotry, operates as gears in the machinery of the economic and social system that governs our lives. As all those who have the least to lose from changing this system get together and examine these social questions, we can separate the wheat of truths from the chaff of old lies. Historic tasks are revealed that beckon us to take a stand and to take action.

That moment is now. And so this conversation with you takes place with the momentum of struggle behind it.

What will it take to put a halt to "legal" and extralegal violence against trans people? How can we strike the unjust and absurd laws mandating dress and behavior for females and males from the books? How can we weed out all the forms of trans-phobic and gender-phobic discrimination?

Where does the struggle for sex and gender liberation fit in relation to other movements for economic and social equality? How can we reach a point where we appreciate each other's differences, not just tolerate them? How can we tear down the electrified barbed wire that has been placed between us to keep us separated, fearful and pitted against each other? How can we forge a movement that can bring about profound and lasting change – a movement capable of transforming society?

These questions can only be answered when we begin to organize together, ready to struggle on each other's behalf. Understanding each other will compel us as honest, caring people to fight each other's oppression as though it was our own.

This book is one of my contributions to this societal discussion. Many of the chapters are adaptations of talks I gave in the spring of 1997, as I set out on the rocky road to recover my health. In the weeks after the last intravenous tubes were removed from my arms and chest, I emerged from illness like a resistance fighter climbing up from a sewer into the sunlight. I faced a calendar filled with opportunities to speak with people at universities, conferences, and rallies. That particular spring was a precious gift I could not take for granted. I'd fought so hard to live.

I remember the enormous physical effort it took to lug my suitcase off a conveyor belt, to walk long distances through crowded airports. But I also remember amazing conversations I had with many wonderful individuals. I found people were ready to talk about sex and gender liberation in every part of the United States I visited – from Manhattan to Tallahassee, from Birmingham to Denver. I was moved by the emotional and enthusiastic responses I received from audiences in Berlin, Leipzig, Köln, and Hamburg, Germany.

Some of those speeches are included in this book. I've prefaced them with a description of the circumstances, audiences, and surroundings, so that you can feel yourself a part of it. I've also included the voices of other trans people — each of whom I deeply respect. These trans people have different identities, experiences, and viewpoints from mine, so you can hear the wider conversation that is now underway.

The poet Rainer Maria Rilke wrote, "Be conversant with transformation." This book is my voice in this conversation. I look forward to hearing yours.

2.

*A*s I stood at the podium to deliver the luncheon keynote at the 9th annual Texas "T" (Transgender) Party in Richardson, Texas, I faced 350 heterosexual cross-dressed males and their spouses. I was the only person in a suit and tie in a room filled with people in dresses. For me, it was an emotionally moving and beautiful moment. I am a cross-dresser. In that sense, I was brother to a room filled with my sisters — male and female. The oppression battled by my spouse, Minnie Bruce, was also deeply understood by those in this room.

One aspect of what makes the annual Texas "T" Party so important is that it brings together bi-gender cross-dressers and their partners — a vast, hidden segment of humanity submerged by oppression.

But the Texas "T" makes another essential contribution. It creates a safe space to bring together people whose lives have been lived in isolation and fear. That's a monumental feat. Part of what made the event feel so safe was that the organizers did such a great job winning over the hotel staff that all the workers wore Texas "T" ribbons and were warm and welcoming to us throughout our stay.

This event offers us the puberty and senior prom we missed. And it's a weeklong model of a society in which gender freedom is defended. The Texas "T" is a remarkable achievement that may enjoy more recognition for its contributions from generations to come than we realize today.

This event is largely carried out through the labor and strength of three organizers — Linda Phillips, Cynthia Phillips, and Bonnie "B." Cynthia and Bonnie were born female. Linda lives full-time as a woman. Linda and Cynthia have been married for 40 years. They share an extraordinary love that is visibly robust. For nine years these three remarkable people have worked like oxen to pull off these successful events. Linda and Cynthia also manage to run the Boulton and Park Society for heterosexual male cross-dressers, issue a regular newsletter, and maintain a Web site.

Most of the cross-dressers who attend this event might be described as bi-gender, meaning they have two important components of their identity — a feminine and a masculine side. A few may identify as bisexual, or would prefer to live as out, full-time transgenderists, or secretly dream of sex-reassignment. However, it is necessary to accept that there are tens of thousands of people in this country — perhaps millions — who want to express both a masculine and a feminine side — and many, many of those people are heterosexual.

Like closeted lesbian, gay, and bisexual people, a large segment of the bi-gender population has lived in airless, confining closets of shame. That's another reason I knew I was in a room with people who understood my own oppression. We did not all have to articulate the guilt, humiliation, or fear of sexual violence that had marred our lives. It was verbalized in our body language; it shone in our eyes.

I knew that the day after this keynote, when suitcases were packed and hotel rooms paid for, when the dresses and the wigs were hidden in luggage, that many of the people in this room would appear to be very different. They would stand around the breakfast atrium in jeans and chinos and two-piece suits. To a casual observer, they might look like other masculine men.

But when this event ends, tears will stream down the cheeks of many of these men. A few will sob because they are going home to a wrenching divorce. Their wives, who did not attend this joyful event, could no longer live with the isolation and the oppression. Others will weep because these are the only days out of their entire lives that they could be themselves — and the event is over.

If you looked at their hands you would see that it is so painful for these males to pack away half of their gender expression — one-half of who they are as human beings — that many will not have removed their red nail polish. When nail polish remover has erased the last visible trace of their transgender, will they be distinguishable from other masculine men? The pain and shame will still linger in the way some hold their bodies, or drop their eyes during conversations. But with others you might never know. What an important reminder that there are a lot of assumptions we make everyday about people based solely on whether they are female or male. Assumptions about consciousness, experience, relationship to oppression, and potential as allies. And those presumptions are not always true.

As I looked out over the Texas "T" audience, I thought about what it was that I wanted to stress. There were two things. First, that women's oppression can't be effectively fought without incorporating the battle against gender oppression. The two systems of oppression are intricately linked. And the populations of women and trans people overlap.

I believe that the lives of many of the cross-dressers and their spouses at this event will be enriched by drawing experience and consciousness from the women's movement. While many males in society think of females as inferior, many of the cross-dressing males at this event think of women as superior. They idealize women and put them on a pedestal. Of course, some women also glorify what it means to be a woman.

But the oppression of women and trans people in this society has led many of us to the same questions. What does it mean to be a woman or a man? Is that different from being female or male? How many variations of sex and gender expression exist? How many of those permutations are socially punished? How do those forms of oppression affect consciousness?

The answers to those questions will be very valuable for both our movements. So one message I wanted to bring to this gathering was the importance of building alliances between the women's and trans liberation movements.

But there was another message I wanted to deliver that I thought was of paramount importance at this historical moment: The lives of lesbians, gays, and bisexuals overlap with the lives of trans people of all sexualities. I was facing an audience who had been told all their lives that men who wore dresses were drag queens who were sexually attracted to men. I knew these heterosexual cross-dressers risked losing the women partners they loved because of this societal assumption that they are gay.

My own life and consciousness straddles the trans communities and the lesbian, gay, and bi communities. I can feel the muscle we could flex if we could fight back together against all forms of discrimination, bigotry, and bashing. And I wanted each person in this room — cross-dresser and partner alike — to feel the potential strength of that coalition.

And so as I began to speak, unity was the most important issue on my mind. The room grew quiet. Food service workers slipped out of the kitchen to listen. No ice clinked in glasses; no forks clanked on plates. As I talked about the connections between our lives, virtually the only sound was of soft sobs as some partners cried quietly into their napkins or on each other's shoulders.

· · ·

Please allow me to introduce myself. My name is Leslie Feinberg – you can call me Les. I am a masculine, lesbian, female-to-male cross-dresser and transgenderist. Because I was raised as a female in this woman-hating society, my consciousness has been shaped by some of the experiences that girls and women of all nationalities generally share in the dominant society. In addition, being a very masculine female has also subjected me to experiences that neither non-trans women or men face.

I support the right of all people to self-determination of their own bodies. I am a resolute ally in defense of transsexual women and men and intersexuals, and in the struggle for women's rights to reproductive freedom. However, I do not personally identify as a man, so I don't believe I should have to change my body to "match" my gender expression so that the authorities can feel comfortable.

Being a masculine female means I am uni-gendered, not bi-gendered. So I have been "out" all my life. That places me – like millions of other masculine females and feminine males – in the social category of "pronoun-challenged." Please feel free to refer to me as "he" in this transgender setting, since in doing so you are honoring my gender expression.

Outside the trans communities, many people refer to me as "she," which is also correct. Using that pronoun to describe me challenges generalizations about how "all women" act and express themselves. In a non-trans setting, calling me "he" renders my transgender invisible.

I would like to live in a world in which I would be described as "Les Feinberg." But I live in a society in which I will never fit either of the little stick figures on public bathroom signs, and I cannot shoehorn myself into either the "M" or "F" box on document applications. Does the "M" or "F" on a driver's license mean Male or Female, Masculine or Feminine? Those who created the M-or-F boxes may think the two are one and the same, since the contemporary dictate is that females will grow up to be feminine and boys to be masculine. But we in this room are all living proof of the gender variance that exists in our society and societies throughout human history.

So I – and millions like me – are caught in a social contradiction. It's legally accurate to check off the "F" on my driver's license permit. But imagine if a state trooper stops me for a taillight violation. He (they have always been he in my experience) sees an "F" on my license but when he shines his flashlight on my face he sees an "M." Now I'm in the middle of a nightmare over a traffic infraction. So I marked down "M" on my driver's license application for my own safety. I can be fined and jailed for that simple checkmark with my pen.

I am someone who loves to travel. There isn't a single spot on this planet I don't long to see and explore. But the M-or-F boxes on passport applications kept me under virtual "house arrest" in this country for most of my life.

So I called the State Department official in charge of the categories on passports and asked her what transgender people like myself were supposed to do. She said if I could provide letters from a psychiatrist and a surgeon detailing that I was a transsexual man and had completed genital surgery, I could check off the "M" box. I explained that this policy was the result of an important legal victory won by transsexual men and women, but it did not apply to millions of us who were transgender.

I added that unless the State Department required the same letters from all passport applicants, this was in effect an illegal strip search of trans people. She replied that I had to check off the "F" box for my own protection because it was based on how passport agents saw my sex.

Well, based on that tidbit, I decided to see how passport agents did view me. I was lucky enough to get one of the new short-form birth certificates. As states transfer information from handwritten birth records to computer, some offer short forms that only include name, date, and place of birth. (I am aware that this is only helpful to those with gender ambiguous birth names.)

I checked off the "M" box on my application and handed it to the passport agency clerk. She looked at me, processed my application, and two weeks later my passport arrived in the mail – as male.

I became a felon at the same time. It's actually a felony to check off the "M" box if you were born female. But I'm not afraid. If I am arrested at any time because of my identification papers, I'll let our communities everywhere know. We are all vulnerable where our identification documents are concerned. I think we could make a hell of a fight out of such an arrest by demanding the M-or-F boxes be removed from documents like passports and driver's licenses.

Authorities like to say such rules cannot be changed. But when I was a kid, I was required to put down my race on documents. That was mandatory – until the Civil Rights and Black liberation movements challenged the racist underpinnings. Then the authorities were forced to remove the "race" box.

What I want to know is why do we have to have an M-or-F box on an application for a document that has a photo? Isn't that the most complex and compelling form of identification? Passport agents don't need a description of anyone's genitals or gender identity. They are just empowered to determine that the traveler and passport match. There's no reason, for example, that a bi-gender person cannot be issued two pieces of identification with photos that reflect both aspects of who they are. I think this is just one example of the ways that communities who don't share the same identities can join in a common struggle for change that will benefit everyone.

That's really the single point I want to stress today. I am a gay, female, cross-dressing transgenderist. I believe that I – and my communities – can be important allies for you as heterosexual cross-dressers and partners. The only question is: Have we reached the moment in history where this dialogue between our communities can begin?

Misconceptions have been a barrier between our communities. In order to have any real dialogue, it means we must all listen carefully to each other. I eagerly read every bit of writing I can find – from *Gender Euphoria* to *Renaissance* to *Monmouth Ocean County Transgender Newsletter* – to listen to your communities in order to understand more. Yet in conversations last night with cross-dressers and partners, I learned still more.

I've also heard many misunderstandings about lesbian and gay cross-dressers. I think that is natural. All of us have been given a textbook definition that, unlike drag queens, heterosexual cross-dressers are "normal in every other way." Many of us have been taught to identify ourselves by what we are not. But it's not a satisfying definition and almost always hurts the people we are defining away from. I believe we should strive for positive self-definition and also defend each other's self-identification as rigorously as we do our own.

Let me try to explain a little about the misunderstandings about lesbian and gay cross-dressers that I hear in this society, from my own point of view. I know that many think of *sexuality* as the organizing drive of lesbian and gay cross-dressing communities. That's not completely true. In actuality, our gender expression has been the primary driving force of cohesion.

The gay and lesbian drag communities – particularly those of us who are uni-gender – have always been "out." We are hounded virtually everywhere we go in public because of our gender expression. So we created collective forms of organization that were relatively public and "above-ground." The gay bars I first discovered in the 1960s in Buffalo, Niagara Falls, and southern Ontario were also transgender bars. They were filled with masculine females, feminine males, and our partners – who had their own highly stylized gender expression. A masculine female was referred to as "butch"; a feminine male as a "queen." If we cross-dressed, we were referred to as "drag."

Drag queens and drag kings are gay and lesbian cross-dressers.

There are bi-gendered lesbian and gay cross-dressers. But those of us who were uni-gendered fought back alone in public everywhere we went. So the only relief we could find was with each other and those who loved us. Our love was illegal – and still is in many states – and our gender expression made us outlaws, too. So we forged alliances, friendships, support, and love in community. The bars were not a peaceful, safe haven. They could be raided at any moment by cops or gangs. But we found relative safety in numbers in public. That fact has shaped our drag cultures dramatically.

Many people in this society have been taught that drag queens and drag kings exaggerate femininity and masculinity to the point of caricature. I vehemently disagree. You can find many styles and degrees of gender expression within the lesbian and gay drag communities. But each person's expression of their gender or genders is their own and equally beautiful. To refer to anyone's gender expression as exaggerated is insulting and restricts gender freedom.

If it is true that drag queens as a whole represent a larger percentage of high-femme expression – and I'm not sure that is a fact – there may be other factors to explain it. The public organization of gay drag life has attracted masculine females and feminine males who are brutally oppressed because of the degree of their gender expression.

And the gay drag community has been a space to explore self-expression. During puberty, most non-trans people had an opportunity to develop their self-expression, shaped in part by social feedback. Many trans people – straight, bisexual, and gay – never had that experience. Their self-expression emerged in isolation. So the gay drag community became the trunk in the attic filled with dresses and ties, boas and fedoras, high heels and wing-tip brogues. It became a place to try on your dreams in front of a community mirror and see if they fit.

And the gay drag community is so ferociously oppressed that high-femme and stone butch expression are also signs of courageous defiance – "I am not altering myself by an atom, no matter what you say or do to me!" That was the message that drag queens and drag kings delivered to the police who raided the Stonewall bar in New York City in June 1969. The raid ignited a four-night-long rebellion against police brutality. And that uprising, in turn sparked the gay liberation movement.

There is another factor that impacts on gender expression in drag culture. Some gay transgenderists found a way to scrape together a living and still be themselves by working in theater. Trans expression has shaped theater, and in turn theater – including modern vaudeville, burlesque, and Broadway – has left its imprint on many gay drag cultures. It has given those of us who walk through the world feeling despised the freedom to perform before cheering, appreciative audiences. Drag queens appear on stage dressed with spectacular flair and panache, wearing sequins and feathers, as do many female performers. As drag kings, we often performed in tuxedoes and tails. No one expects performance artists – from Judy Garland to Fred Astaire – to appear on stage in jeans and sneakers, or other everyday clothing.

I never describe anyone's gender expression as exaggerated. Since I don't accept negative judgments about my own gender articulation, I avoid judgments about others. People of all sexes have the right to explore femininity, masculinity – and the infinite variations between – without criticism or ridicule.

We, as cross-dressers – gay, bisexual, and straight – and our partners, have a stake in challenging restrictive attitudes toward human behavior and self-expression. And I believe that combating every form of prejudice against lesbian, gay, and bisexual love has importance for all of us here, as well.

For example, there's a snake lurking in the definition that "straight cross-dressers, unlike drag queens, are normal in every other way" that will bite you if you reach for it. Does that mean that you or your partner are not "normal" some of the time? No! I am looking at wonderful, courageous human beings.

I want to stress that I understand there is a unique and awesome pressure that has made it difficult for us as gay and straight cross-dressers to get together to talk about our differences and similarities. And that is because cross-dressing has always been socially synonymous with gayness. I think this misconception is based on the fact that uni-gender lesbian and gay cross-dressers were socially visible and organized at a time when most bi-gender, heterosexual cross-dressers were isolated or members of "underground" organizations.

So I want to talk to you about what I think is the deepest problem that has kept us apart. And if I make mistakes, please understand that I am still learning about your lives.

I understand the rage you must feel when someone claims that your identity is an expression of shame – that you are gay and won't admit it. And I have thought a lot lately about what it must feel like to have one person in the world who loves you. Who you yearn for sexually. And who you fear will spurn you and leave you if they mistakenly think that your sexuality has changed – that you must be gay.

I talked about how the gay cross-dressing community has been shaped by being an above-ground, community-based group. But the heterosexual cross-dressing experience has all too often been shaped in isolation. I can barely allow myself to imagine the loneliness of a male who can only see her feminine reflection in a motel mirror in a strange town twice a year. The pain of a husband who thinks to herself everyday – my wife *thinks* she loves me, but she doesn't know the *real* me. Would she still love me if she knew? Would she stay?

I have followed the discussion in your community about the ethics of telling or not telling your wives and partners. It is not my place to take a position in that internal debate.

I say to the wives here, I can understand how the disclosure after many years of intimacy can feel like a betrayal to you. But think about how deeply your spouse loves you for him to so fear losing you. You mean the world to us. For some of us, you are the only comfort and love and safety we have ever known. I feel nothing but compassion for both partners. In a society in which people could be themselves without fear of loss, humiliation, or brutality, who would not reveal themselves fully to the ones they love?

Of course you as cross-dressers have needed to stress to your wives over and over again that you are revealing twin aspects of your *gender* expression. That your *sexuality* has not changed. Perhaps there is a way to do that without using the phrase "I'm not gay" because those are such loaded words in an anti-gay society. I think what you are really trying to say is "You have been and you still are the person I desire." We all need to help in creating new words and concepts that say who we are, not who we aren't.

And to the partners: What language is there for you? How do you deal with your gender preference for a masculine sexual partner, when your husband reveals a feminine side to you? How does that change the ways you express your sexuality? For you also it's important to have fresh ways to think about yourself and your bond of sexuality with your partner. Some wives I have talked to tell me that their partner's disclosure means they have to consider whether they are in a lesbian relationship. Others are exploring their own gender expression; some have also begun cross-dressing.

Wouldn't it be wonderful if we could all support the understanding that gender expression does not determine sexuality, and then open up a discussion between our communities? Many in this room could benefit from being able to sit in workshops with lesbian and gay and bisexual cross-dressers and partners, and talk about how to free human sexuality from the paradigm that heterosexuality is normal and same-sex love is not.

After all, you may be legally married, but to Jesse Helms two partners in identical lingerie are not straight!

We have all been wounded in the ways we negotiate sex and intimacy; we fear communicating our needs and desires. Greater freedom to conceive the limitless potential of human sexuality, without shame, is an important and necessary contribution to all of humanity.

And we need more language than just feminine/masculine, straight/gay, either/or. Men are not from Mars and women are not from Venus. We all live on the same planet. The "separate planet" theories have been used to justify the discrimination, violence, and inequality women face. Everything that supports such spurious "theories" must be called into question. We need to refocus on defending the diversity in the world that already exists, and creating room for even more possibilities.

A person who lives as another gender – whether in a motel room twice a year or in a marriage, a flight of fantasy or a gay bar – challenges what it means to be male or female, what it means to be a man or a woman. Our partners share that confrontation. What is manliness or womanliness? What to keep? What to reject? Is there just one road to woman or to man? Is it common experience for African-American and white cross-dressers? Female-to-male or male-to-female cross-dressers? Corporate executive or sales clerk?

When we find the courage to live openly as who we are – trans people and partners – we begin a wild roller coaster ride. The weight of difficulties we endure as a result of our decision is a constant reminder of the unwavering force of social gravity. And no longer being tracked into "gender-appropriate" behavior and dress sends us hurtling into freefall because we are no longer able to easily define ourselves or our relationship to others.

But what a ride! Even at gunpoint, I would not choose a different path in life. My determination to remain a person who I can be proud of has made all of my views and insights and consciousness possible. It has made me see more clearly how many other lives in society are being limited through forms of discrimination and injustice. It has illuminated my relationship to them as an ally, and steeled my resolve to spend my life actively working for a world in which economic and social equality, and freedom of self-expression, are the birthrights of every person.

We as cross-dressers don't have to explain *why* we are the way we are. We have to explain *who* we are. How we see ourselves.

And you, the wives, are an extraordinary group of women with individual qualities of bravery and insight that can shape the way all women look at themselves. You had to reexamine everything you were taught about what it means to be a woman when your partner joined you by taking her first wobbly steps on high heels down that road together. We need you in the ranks of the women's liberation movement, too!

Personally, I would also benefit from expanding concepts and language of gender possibilities. In rooms outside of these, it is necessary to describe myself in terms of a simplified social equation: I was born female, and my gender expression is masculine. For that reason, my birth sex and my gender expression appear to be at odds. I believe this is a social contradiction that can only exist in a society that mandates — with coercive force — that gender expression must conform to birth biology.

I do not champion the idea that we are each born completely biologically hardwired for life. I don't think of my biology as a fixed constellation, or as the only star that steers my life's course. On the other hand, I don't endorse the belief that I am merely a blank slate, following societal instructions. I don't refer to my own self-expression as a role or a part that I have learned by rote through simple memorization of societal rules. If that were true, my trans identity could be explained away as merely an inability to learn.

The modern premise that we are born already completely coded for all our complex sexual responses and gender expression embodies similar dangers for the lesbian, gay, bisexual communities and the trans communities.

I think that the race involved in the genome project – which is a rather polite term for the land-grab, patenting, and private ownership of the genes that are the building blocks of human life – has been accompanied by its own form of Jurassic Park public relations. I view science as the priceless legacy of humanity's search for understanding of the material world. But in an unequal economic system, science cannot avoid being stained by prevailing prejudices and bigotry – not only social sciences, like anthropology, but the so-called hard sciences like biology.

For example, look at all the hoopla about the gay hypothalamus. The discovery of somewhat smaller hypothalami, in a few brains labeled gay, resulted in a media popularization that reduced the findings to a kind of bully-boy schoolyard boast that "my hypothalamus is bigger than yours."

But were the brains that were labeled gay those of men who were attracted to other men for their entire lives without exception? And how do we know if the "heterosexual" brains were really so straight? Could scientists really go back and rule out that college weekend, or that hunting trip with a good buddy? The whole search for a gay gene is predicated on the hypothesis that human beings can be so easily and so rigidly partitioned into either "straight" or "gay."

One of the great gifts of the Kinsey report, which most of us in this room remember, was that it revealed that even in a society where the coercive and punitive powers of the state are wielded to repress same-sex desire, those who identify as exclusively hetero-sexual or homosexual for their entire lives are in a minority. Like a rainbow of new information after a storm of suppression, Kinsey revealed the iridescent hues of human sexuality.

So how can we not be suspect of scientific findings that don't ask: What size is a bisexual hypothalamus? Let alone the question of whether the limitless variations of same-sex fantasy and desire can really be solely ruled by a chromosome rocking in a chemical ocean.

And doesn't the fact that sexual passion between two men or two women is illegal in many states affect both the premise and the inter-pretations of such research projects? Are the fears of some lesbian women and gay men that the search for a gay gene will lead to a eugenics campaign to eradicate this aspect of human sexuality unfounded?

The search for a gay gene in a society in which gay and lesbian love is illegal and brutalized is about as "objective" as a scientific study of potential differences between Jewish and Gentile brains would be if it was conducted in Germany during the rise of fascism.

I feel it's possible to say that at this moment in time, our destinies are determined by the constant interaction between the ship we are fitted with, the direction we set for ourselves, and the forces in society that affect our course – including the gale winds of bigotry, the undertow of discrimination, and the deeply carved channels of poverty and inequality.

The "nature versus nurture" debate has meaning for each of us here because we are constantly being asked in life: Why are you the way you are? When did you first know you were different? Do you think that while you were in the womb your tiny fist inadvertently clenched an essential gene too hard? Or was your mother domineering?

And my answer is: Who cares! As long as my right to explore the full measure of my own potential is being trampled by discriminatory laws, as long as I am being socially and economically marginalized, as long as I am being scapegoated for the crimes committed by this economic system, my right to exist needs no explanation or justification of any kind.

More sex and gender variation exists among human beings than can be answered by the simplistic question I'm hit with every day of my life: Are you a man or a woman?

I can speak more complexly about myself here because of the amount of time we in this room have spent pondering questions of self-expression. I would say that I was born with physical characteristics that – within my particular ethnicity, nationality, class, region, and historical period – were not considered distinctly female. And by the time I had developed fluency in spoken language as a child, and uniquely adapted it to fit my own needs for knowledge and communication, I had also developed a dialect of movement and body language that was considered only appropriate for male articulation.

I watched as masculine girl children like myself – referred to as tomboys – and feminine boys – branded as sissies and pansies – were shamed, threatened, beaten, and terrorized into conforming to a pinker or a bluer tint of gender. Many of the accommodations they adapted as teenagers – longer or shorter hair, a practiced swagger or sway, or an exaggerated public exhibition of hetero-sexuality – did little to conceal their forbidden gender expression, but instead twisted their whole beings into a countenance of self-loathing and defeat.

Others, like myself, either could not or would not conform. Our wounds are deep and clearly visible, too. I think that's one of the reasons, as I mentioned before, that butch females and feminine males are sometimes accused of gender overstatement. I would call it a courageous gender confrontation. And since the world is such a dangerous place for us wherever we go, and the violence is so intense that few of us live out our full lifespans, there is little time or room for gender development or gender layering.

I am lucky to have survived to the age of 47. Last year I was very close to death, needlessly, because of bigotry and lack of money. The instances where I was treated with hatred and denied emer-gency health care were based on one obvious fact: I am a masculine female. I am perceived as trying to look or act "like a man." I actu-ally think that's a very limiting concept that endangers the rights of any female or male to a range of gender choices.

I actually feel that on my own loom, weaving my internal weft against the warp of external pressure, I have created a tapestry far more intricate and complex.

While there is as yet no language for who I have become, I artic-ulate my gender – silent to the ear, but thunderous to the eye. And that is what determines the depth and breadth of the oppression I battle on the streets virtually every minute of every day. That is the truth of my life that cannot be answered by the simplistic question: Are you a man or a woman?

Yet radio and television interviewers still repeat the same questions to me again and again. "But were you born male or female? Why do you think you are the way you are? Were you born this way? Was your mother overbearing? Did your father want a boy?" These questions have no meaning for me.

I don't think the point is: Why are we different? Why have we refused to walk one of two narrow paths, but instead demanded the right to blaze our own? The question is not why we were unwilling to conform even when being beaten to the ground by ridicule and brutality.

The real burning question is: How did we ever find the courage? From what underground spring did we draw our pride? How did each of us make our way in life, without a single familiar star in the night sky to guide us, to this room where we have at last found others like ourselves? And after so much of ourselves has been injured, or left behind as expendable ballast, many of us worry "What do we have left to give each other? Upon what basis will we build something lasting between us?"

I think we have a whole world to give back to each other.

We have the material to create the strong structures of each of our communities, while still building the foundation for a coalition of our diversity to fight for common goals. If we want to win our own demands, we need allies. And as we fight for each other's rights, we strengthen our own.

When your rights are trampled on, call on us – the lesbian, gay, and bisexual communities. We are your allies.

Picture the lesbian, gay, bisexual, and the trans communities as two huge overlapping circles. Like the drag queens who rebelled at Stonewall, I stand in that overlap, and we can serve as bridges. Let us combine the power of our communities. Stonewall was not just a lesbian and gay rebellion. Stonewall is your historic landmark too.

So I end as I began: My name is Les Feinberg. I am a gay, female, cross-dressing transgenderist. I believe that I – and my communities – can be important allies for you as heterosexual cross-dressers and partners. The only question is: Have we reached the moment in history when this dialogue between our communities can begin?

*"I have actually
had the best of any life
I could dream of"*

Thank you so much for your interest in that part
of my life which encompasses a great deal of my sixty-two years. I have
many people ask me why I changed "sex" when, of course, it was my gender I "changed." When a cross-dresser is young he believes it is all in the
clothes, if he is allowed to experience a change of gender he discovers
clothes had nothing to do with it. However, in the male way we are visual
and the clothes have the ability to let us feel, if only for a short time, what
it must "seem" to feel as the other gender. When we are young we mix
it all up with sex, being full of testosterone and desire. When some of
us get older and begin to understand what this might mean, it can be
terrifying.

There are few men in this world who want to abandon their masculinity, regardless of how they might really feel inside. Being a man is a very
heady thing in our world and, even if you have had to "fake it" as I did for
fifty years, it is a familiar thing and no one wants to leave the familiar to
take a long step down into the other world. Few of my friends who are cds
[cross-dressers] would care to do as I have and, to be frank, it is economic
suicide as well as disturbing to others of your acquaintance.

In my case I always knew what I was regardless of evidence to the contrary between my legs. The awful part came when I realized I was attracted
to women and not men, which I just naturally assumed I would be. Imagine a little girl peering into her mother's mirror wondering where she could
find another little girl who would be interested in her.

Somewhere in the late 1940s, my mother – who kept finding me cross-
dressed, took me to a famous therapist who deemed that I was indeed a

homosexual because I wore girl's clothes. While my mother was upset, I was almost relieved. I knew inside I was a girl but was confused about the sex part. For some time I would wake up in the morning thinking this was the day I would start liking guys. I would furtively glance at the other guys in the boys' shower, but I was disappointed because they looked just like me – not that I wanted to look the way I did – but I was not impressed by all those penises and gawky bodies. I still mooned over the girls; I wanted to not only love them and be with them, I wanted to BE them.

When I started dating, it was my mother's turn to be confused. I started going out when I built my first car at fourteen (two things I loved to do growing up, working on cars and dressing as a girl. Go figure.) I went with all the girls I could go with, almost destroying my health in the process. I found to my delight that girls really liked me; I had the unique ability to understand where they were coming from and truly liked being with them – unlike my male friends who only wanted a quick conquest. I never had a woman turn my advances away, and in most cases it was they who made the first move in a romantic situation. This was because I loved romance and being in love just as they did. The other boys they went out with had none of my finesse.

Sometimes I would tell these girls about myself and the attitudes were mixed; young girls do not usually have fixed opinions about things such as cross-dressing. It is not until they start looking for someone to marry and have a family with that they become concerned with finding a "straight, normal guy." My dating years were happy and full of fun; I even found girls who would allow me to wear their clothes and play bedroom games.

Why the difference between me and my CD friends? One important word: GUILT. I never had it. I knew I had come down the assembly line this way, why worry about it. It was not until I got into the TG [transgender] community that I learned about the terrible way everyone seemed to suffer from guilt. My parents allowed me to just grow up. My mother did not like my cross-dressing, but never told me not to do it – just keep it in the closet so the neighbors wouldn't know. We were not religious people, but I did read the bible. I suppose I never picked up on the admonition to not wear the clothes of the opposite sex and probably would not have paid any attention in any case simply because it was not the clothes I was after, it was the desire to be who I really was.

I didn't know what a lesbian was until I was around seventeen or so. I never figured them to be in the slightest way connected to me – after all, they were still real women and I was not. And the lesbians I came into contact with frightened me; they were so much like the very thing I hated being a male. It was only when I was much older and met a "femme" that I got a glimmer of understanding about these women.

"In this world of ordinary people" was how I was leading my life – when on the only blind date I ever had in my life, I met the person who has made my life the absolute joy it is. One day, after we had known each other a suitable amount of time – around two or three months – I told my lady that I wanted to "win the Indy 500, loved old movies, walks, picnics, and, oh yeah, once in a while I liked to put on a dress and be a girl." Cynthia was not shocked, not upset in any way; she accepted it as she accepted all my oddities. When we fell in love, the gender part simply did not play a large part in it. She has that incredible ability to see into the inner part of a person, their soul. The only jarring note I remember in all this was when she first saw me dressed, she made the deathless remark that I "certainly needed a lot of work!"

When you see me, you see the result of her forty-year effort to make me the lady I wish to be. She never gave up on me. It is not easy to turn a male into a female, either the apparent or the inner part. The mental was the most difficult; no one would begin to imagine how difficult it is to stop thinking as an aggressive, demanding male – the person I had to be in order to survive in a world women can only guess at. Cynthia taught me what I needed to know in order to be what I felt I was, since "wanting" is only a tiny part of accomplishment.

When I was young I had a fear of being found out by my peers so I invented "Jim," a guy that would literally beat the shit out of anyone who looked at him the wrong way. When it was discovered, much later in all this, that "Jim" had become "Linda" I lost 99% percent of the males I had once called friends – not because I was a cross-dresser, but because I had become so totally a woman.

When I was a male I was a straight, aggressive, hard male; when I was a woman I was the complete opposite, no one knew except my lady. When we went out in public with me as Linda no one ever guessed; after all, I had all the expertise and knowledge of one of the most beautiful women in the world at my disposal. She would have never let me out the door if I wasn't as good as I could be. No one laughed, no one pointed, and more importantly to me, no one knew. In those years, cross-dressing was highly illegal. It truly was an era when to be read was to be dead. I was never oppressed because everyone thought of me as the perfect male when I was acting as one, and I was never pointed out as a queen or a cd because I appeared to be a feminine woman who blended in with the other women – because I had someone who looked out for me and made that possible.

True gender lies not in the appearance of the body but the workings of the mind. Cynthia and I have what you might term a monosexual relationship – we really aren't like two lesbians but we aren't like two heterosexuals either. Since the day we met we really have had only eyes for one another and now in the declining years of our lives we find an even greater love for one another. She treats me, much to my delight, as the woman I appear to be. And much to our surprise, I seem to become that woman more so every day. All this makes my life so wonderful it is difficult to imagine.

I wish I could write about the problems of being transgendered, and of course I have had problems with it, but they were really not problems to me, looking back. I have actually had the best of any life I could dream of.

CYNTHIA PHILLIPS

"Our life today is vastly different from when Linda was Jim"

I always have a difficult time trying to explain the relationship between Linda and I. Every-one wants to believe I am either excited about Linda's lifestyle or I am the most tolerant woman in the gender community. Neither is correct.

The fact of Linda being a transgendered person has really not played that large a part in our relationship. When we were young and she told me about it, I knew nothing about any of it. I really wasn't even aware that there were people who were unhappy with their sex (now I would say gender). Linda did not know a lot about what she was at the age of twenty-two either. She was so matter-of-fact in telling me that I was not shocked or upset about it; I just accepted it as a part of someone I was in love with. I felt that Linda was such a fine person that anything she did could not be a bad thing. I always have looked inside a person and have not been concerned about appearance. So when I looked into Linda's (Jim's) soul I saw someone who had the qualities I desired in a person I planned on spending my life with.

Linda says that I have made her the woman she is today, but that is a statement I am not in complete agreement with. All I did was provide a role model for her to be not only a woman but a lady, something that is important to both of us.

Our life today is vastly different from when Linda was Jim. Jim felt, as most men, that if he earned the major part of our income he was not obligated to take part in any of the household chores. He also felt that all his decisions were correct and not to be questioned, a feeling most males have. Now that I have Linda I have someone who not only helps me but who actually seeks and values my opinion.

When Linda went full time, I was a little frightened at the prospect. Now I believe it was the best thing that could have happened to our relationship. She has been able to release the softer side of herself, which she kept bottled up for years. The kind, gentle person I have always known was there is the one I see every day.

CYNTHIA AND LINDA PHILLIPS, THE ORGANIZERS OF THE TEXAS "T" PARTY, CAN BE REACHED AT: P.O. BOX 17, BULVERDE, TEXAS 78163

3.

As Minnie Bruce and I unpacked in our hotel room in Laurel, Maryland, we heard a k.d. lang song playing so loudly it seemed she was crooning just outside our second-floor room. I pulled back the curtains and looked out the windows that opened above a huge indoor atrium with a swimming pool. Below, I could see organizers hard at work setting up hundreds of chairs in an L-shaped pattern with a podium at the point. In just two hours, the True Spirit Conference would begin.

The call for this regional conference had described the event as open to "people who are themselves, or who are supportive of others who were assigned female gender at birth, but who feel that is not an adequate or accurate description of who they are." I had no idea how many people would show up. Organizing for the conference had largely taken place in cyberspace. So in my nervousness, I immersed myself in the small tasks of unpacking and getting dressed.

An hour later, I walked into the atrium. More than 300 people were already crowded into the cavernous room. Excited voices echoed. The room was filled to capacity with human beings who represented a spectrum of sexes and genders. Some described themselves as transsexual men or transmen. Of those, some self-identified as female-to-male (FTM). Others defined themselves as male-to-male (MTM) in recognition of the fact that they had not ever felt female in their lives.

Still others in the audience used FTM or F2M as an adjective, rather than a noun, to describe themselves as female-to-male cross-dressers. Masculine females — some of them identified as butches, drag kings, and tomboys — attended. So did intersexuals and people who identified as a third sex. Some Native people self-identified as Two Spirit, others as True Spirit. Among the trans warriors were those who battled on many fronts because of racism, homophobia, bi-phobia, Deaf and disabled oppressions, sexism and poverty. And parents, lovers, wives, husbands, friends, and allies of trans people — including male-to-female (MTF) transsexual women — packed the audience.

When the moment arrived for me to speak, my legs felt rubbery. This was the first public appearance I'd made since coming off intravenous care. As I stood at the podium, fishing for my reading glasses, I could hear the swoosh of air as the ASL interpreter finished signing my introduction. I signed "Welcome" to the Deaf trans warriors in the front row and began to speak. My voice trembled, registering the toll of illness. The audience grew so quiet that I could hear the lapping of the water in the nearby pool.

It is not unusual for a speaker delivering a conference keynote to characterize the event as historic. But it is not always accurate or true. I feel honored to be asked to speak to you all tonight because, without hyperbole, I believe this conference is a historic milestone.

What is so momentous about this event is *who* the organizers called to gather here. And for this, enormous credit is owed to the conference chairperson, Gary Bowen, and to each organizer for breathing life into the call for unity between diverse peoples.

When I received the first call testing interest in such a conference, the event was loosely referred to as "Transman East." Yet the description of the event included many gender-variant communities. Either conference would make a valuable, but different contribution.

I e-mailed Gary that the call created a question for many of us who are not transmen, but who are part of the F2M spectrum described in the call. I would support a transman conference. But I would not attend out of respect for the right of transmen to their own space to meet and organize. Yet if the conference was striving for a broad reach, but many of us didn't hear that, the resulting conference – sorely needed – would be skewed by our lack of participation.

Gary's immediate response deepened my respect for him as an organizer. Without any defensiveness, he wrote that it was impossible to raise the idea of a conference without calling it something. But that he had indeed envisioned a conference that brought together all the gender variance on what he called the F2M continuum, including our significant others, families, friends, and allies.

Then Gary tackled a problem of language that directly shaped the concept of who was welcome at this conference. Since there's no one word or phrase that is agreed upon for this diverse population, Gary drew on his Apache heritage and offered the creative title for this conference: True to the Spirit Within, or True Spirit.

I'd like to read the call that spelled out who is welcome at this conference, because this inclusion is what makes this event so significant: This conference is open to people "who are themselves, or who are supportive of others who were assigned female gender at birth, but who feel that is not an adequate or accurate description of who they are, which includes but is not limited to: tomboys, butches, female cross-dressers, drag kings, F2MS, transmen, third sexes, intersexuals, and others, along with partners, friends, family and allies."

No one call has ever been issued to organize a gathering of so many of our identities in our own names. And the importance of the words "and others" in this call cannot be overstated. Those two words welcome your own unique and hard-fought-for identity to emerge, to find language and representation. In doing so, you enrich us all.

When I was young, I faced two narrow doorways – female and male. I was told these were the only routes to human expression and experience, predetermined by birth. Each of us here, and the trans movement as a whole, is offering trans children today – all children – a roadmap of choices, and the opportunity to speak to us about what we have found on our journeys. With the vital words "and others" we are protecting uncharted territory, to insure that it remains available for exploration.

This conference, and our trans movement as a whole, honors the contributions and strengths, dignity and courage of all of us as trans people. Each of us is a warrior, or we wouldn't be here tonight. And let us honor the warriors who help make our communities and our lives whole, and without whom our struggle would be much more formidable and arduous. Let's give a standing ovation to those who fight shoulder-to-shoulder with us everyday: our significant others, our friends, our families, and our allies. This conference has been enhanced by their inclusion as equal partners in building it.

Our significant others are not observers of "our" oppression. They are not "related" to our movement. All of our significant others are partners in the life-changing experience of trans consciousness and struggle.

We must challenge the misconception that transmen are automatically typecast as masculine and so their partners must automatically be feminine women. The entire range of gender expression can be found in the transmale population, including androgynous and feminine men, and drag queens. And the transmale community includes many gay and bisexual men, as well as heterosexuals. The courage of gay and bi transmen and their partners to be out and proud and define their sexuality generates a shower of sparks that electrifies the potential of human sexuality.

We also need to defend the rights of transsexual men and their partners to remain active members in other communities. Those of us who bridge the lesbian, gay, bi, women's, and trans communities have a responsibility to educate and agitate for the rights of transmen and their partners who helped build those communities. They deserve the option of retaining their roots and networks of support during periods of changing self-definition, transitions with partners, and sex reassignment. No one who has pitched in to build and defend women's and lesbian, gay, bi liberation is a "traitor" because of who they love, or because they have transitioned from female to male.

And all sexually oppressed communities benefit from the social and personal insights gleaned from supporting the transitions of transmen and transwomen.

Building unity also places the task of fighting sexism on all of us. That statement is not an attack on those of us who were born female, but express ourselves as masculine or male. Sexism is the enemy of every human being. No matter where you place yourself on the sex and gender continua, the degradation, depisal, and unequal treatment of all who are "not male" is an obstacle to solidarity.

Everyone on the F2M spectrum – no matter how you define that term – challenges the narrow definition of male as a person born with a penis, who has "biologically determined" masculinity and an innate sexual desire for women. Sexism – built into this economic and social system – seeks to narrow how men define and express themselves. Those ideas limit individual potential, and therefore all human potential.

But we are reexamining many social ideas surrounding the modern Western concept of "man." What does it mean to be a man? How many different ways are there for men to express their gender, their sexuality, their attitudes toward each other, and the ways they relate to those who are not male or masculine? This important contribution by all F2Ms brings insights and new freedom of self-definition and expression to all men – to all people – in our society.

The struggles of those of us at this conference also overlap with the struggles of the women's liberation movement. We could gain strength by working together, along with all our allies, to fight for sex and gender freedom. That means the rights of people to define their sex, control their own body, and develop their gender expression free from violence, economic barriers, or discrimination – in employment, housing, health care, or any other sector of society.

None of us can ever be free while others are still in chains. That's the truth underlying the need for solidarity. Trans liberation is inextricably linked to other movements for equality and justice.

For example, when the second wave of the women's liberation movement in this country challenged the patriarchal ruling class – thereby threatening the profits they extract from women's inequality – those powers conducted a campaign to discredit the demands of women. Every tool of mass communication delivered a message to men, and to women not yet drawn into the movement, that these uppity women were trying to destroy the "sacred differences" between men and women.

When women urged passage of such a basic, modest piece of legislation as the Equal Rights Amendment, Phyllis Schlafley tried to scare audiences. She predicted that passage of the bill would force men and women to use unisex toilets. If you ask me, I think most people – especially transgender folk – would feel a lot safer and more comfortable if the signs read "Toilet" and the rooms were single-occupancy, clean, sanitary, and had a lock on the door.

Schlafley also argued that, "Equal rights for women will make homosexual marriages legal." Wow, that sounds like reason enough to pass the ERA! Our trans communities are still defending our already existing same-sex marriages. And we're uniting with lesbian, gay, and bisexual activists to win legal and social benefits for all marriages and all families. Whether or not you personally want to get married, this is a progressive fight against blatant discrimination by the state, like the struggles to defeat racist miscegenation laws that banned interracial marriages.

But in recent years, the women's liberation movement has been slowed by a period of deep reaction, including stepped-up attacks attempting to make a mockery of the gains of the women's, lesbian, gay, bisexual, and other progressive movements.

One such perversion of the gains of our movements is the right-wing reversal of the meaning of *politically correct*. When the movements were in full stride, being politically correct was a good thing. It meant confronting racist, sexist, anti-Semitic, homophobic, anti-disabled, and anti-worker slurs, attitudes, and actions. It meant using language that demonstrated respect and sensitivity for each other's oppression.

George Bush, and later Rush Limbaugh, waged a divisive campaign to use that phrase against the movements as a weapon. Their ilk asks: "Why do we have to all be so 'politically correct?'" What they mean is why can't they publicly repeat the crude, bigoted slurs they used before these movements challenged them. The right wing has characterized these progressive movements as "oppressors." The message from those in power is: Don't blame us, blame the people trying to change the situation. This is an attempt to thwart the formation of new liberation movements. But these movements are potential allies, not enemies.

Of course, revealing the need for solidarity takes patient education. But we have made great strides in a short time. For example, I have seen a substantial current of women across the United States—straight, lesbian, and bisexual—welcome discovering more about trans liberation. They are thrilled at the way our movement is helping revitalize women's liberation by revisiting discussions about what it means to be a woman, and how the reduction of "woman" to one common experience is transphobic, as well as insensitive to racism, poverty, disabilities, and other forms of multiple oppression.

And I hope everyone saw the results of the recent *Advocate* magazine poll. Sixty-four percent of those polled said gay and lesbian civil rights groups should make an effort to support the cause of transgender rights. Thirteen percent said they weren't sure—we've got to reach them!

Not every single person in every movement will be won over to the need for trans solidarity. Movements are made up of people like us, who are set in motion by anger at injustice. Rallies, picket lines, and marches provide the opportunity for individuals who have struggled against their oppression alone – often without language to express their experience – to open up conversations with hundreds, thousands of others who have faced similar experiences. That offers potential for awakening consciousness.

But just because an individual is drawn into the vortex of a movement, it doesn't mean that person will automatically be enlightened on every aspect of other peoples' oppressions – particularly that which they do not directly experience. Each individual still needs to overcome the bigotry that has been instilled in us from an early age. A gay man does not necessarily see the need to fight sexism automatically; a white transperson doesn't automatically see the need to fight racism. But the progressive momentum inherent in movements offers a greater potential for individuals to gain an understanding of the struggles of others – particularly in coalitions.

The movements that came before us offer us a legacy of victories – and valuable lessons to keep us from repeating the same mistakes. For example, the U.S. suffragists did have a wing that took up questions of transgender, particularly cross-dressing. Dr. Mary Walker, a female-to-male cross-dresser, played an important role, as did others.

But all white suffragists did not understand the necessity of uniting against slavery. The great abolitionist, writer, and orator Frederick Douglass did understand the need to weld the power of these two movements. Douglass steadfastly defended the right of women to vote. He was one of 31 men at the first Women's Rights convention at Seneca Falls, New York. The men who attended were attacked by enemies of women's suffrage as "Aunt Nancy Men" and "Hermaphrodites"—transphobic and anti-intersexual epithets. Douglass was the only man to address that convention. He declared that women's suffrage was a right, and he said, "Our doctrine is that right is of no sex." Those words still hold great truth for the trans and women's movements today.

A few years before he died, Douglass told the International Council of Women, "When I ran away from slavery, it was for myself; when I advocated emancipation, it was for my people; but when I stood up for the rights of women, self was out of the question, and I found a little nobility in the act." Unfortunately, one of the great mistakes of the dominant current of the nineteenth-century women's liberation movement was that it did not rise to that nobility, did not see the necessity of uniting the fight for women's suffrage with all out combat against slavery and racism. Wings of movements can make mistakes—in this case grievous.

The second wave of women's liberation in the 1970s was made up of many currents, including women of color, socialist feminists, and others, who fought for an understanding that all women don't face identical oppression. Many white women within the movement recognized the necessity to be on the frontlines against racism.

This wave of women's liberation also provided a deeper understanding of the mechanisms by which women and men are differently and unequally socialized in society. And the women's movement revealed that many concepts about masculinity and femininity are designed as justifications of inequality. Masculinity is defined as strong, courageous, and rational. Femininity is defined as the opposite of those characteristics.

Many in the movement who yearned not only for women's liberation, but also for human liberation, embarked on a bold social experiment. They hoped that freeing individuals from femininity and masculinity would help people be viewed on a more equal basis that highlighted each person's qualities and strengths. They hoped that androgyny would replace masculinity and femininity and help do away with gendered expression altogether.

Twenty years after that social experiment, we have the luxury of hindsight. The way in which individuals express themselves is a very important part of who they are. It is not possible to force all people to live outside of femininity and masculinity. Only androgynous people live comfortably in that gender space. There's no social compulsion powerful enough to force anyone else to dwell there. Trans people are an example of the futility of this strategy. Mockery and beatings and unemployment and hunger and threats of rape and institutionalization have not forced us as trans people to conform to narrow norms.

Why would we want to ask anyone to give up their own hard-fought-for place on the gender spectrum? There are no rights or wrongs in the ways people express their own gender style. No one's lipstick or flattop is hurting us. No one's gender expression is any more "liberated" than anyone else's.

Gender freedom — isn't that what we're all fighting for with every breath we take? Well, how are we going to win it if we don't support each other's right to be different from us? Each person has the right to express their gender in any way that feels most comfortable — masculine or feminine, androgynous, bi- and tri-gender expression, gender fluidity, gender complexity, and gender contradiction. There are many shades of gender that are not even represented in language yet. One could argue that leather people and nuns are their own genders.

People don't have to give up their individuality or their particular manner of gender expression in order to fight sex and gender oppression. It's just the opposite. People won't put their time, energy, and commitment into organizing unless they know that the movement they are building is defending their lives.

By bringing together so many gender-variant people, we will be much more equipped to discuss and expose how many of the social values attached to masculinity and femininity are harmful. Gender expression does not determine the abilities, or lack of abilities, in any individual. Those concepts leave us all in harm's way.

For example, femininity – in females and in males – is despised and oppressed in this misogynist society. We've all heard statements like: "The tighter the skirt the looser the morals. The higher the heels the lower the IQ. No one dressed like that could possibly have any self-pride or consciousness. If she, or he, was going to wear a dress like that they should have known they were inviting rape."

This hatred of everything that is feminine is the distilled essence of anti-woman attitudes.

The women's movement is right – females are socialized very differently and unequally. But the trans movement reveals a more layered and complex socialization process. Does a masculine girl absorb social education about what it means to be a "girl" in the same way as a feminine girl? Does a feminine boy grow up identifying with, or fearing, the masculine boys learning to swagger and take up space? How does a transsexual child or adult absorb the messages of how a "real" man or woman is supposed to act and relate?

· · ·

Here we are in a room together – hundreds of trans people and those who love and support us. It's like a dream come true to those of us who grew up in a cold sweat of terror because we feared we were the only person in the world who was different. We were isolated in this society. We did not see our lives represented in television and the movies – except in the most degrading and dehumanizing fashion. We were isolated by difference in a society that demanded conformity. We longed to find others like ourselves. We yearned for friendship and understanding.

Tonight we are together – some of us for the first time – with others "like ourselves." And yet, we are not the same. In fact, it took a whole paragraph and the words "and others" to bring us all here tonight. We don't describe ourselves in the same ways, see ourselves in the same ways. We come from different cultures and backgrounds and experiences. Collectively we reside on a span of identities.

And so if we really want that friendship and that understanding, we have to build it. All of us in this society are wounded. But we don't always know where each other's injuries are located. That means we may thoughtlessly hurt each other. Everyone who has ever been treated unjustly or been disrespected in this society is full of justified anger. I believe we need to take care not to unleash that rage on each other.

Our identities have been reduced to caricatures in the dominant culture. As a result, we all harbor misunderstandings about each other. But I don't think the problems are insurmountable for this reason: We need each other. We each know what it's like to fight back alone. We need each other's strength as allies. And we know what it's like to feel like the only one who's different. When "difference" suddenly comes into focus as diversity it's a healing experience. There are people in this room who are ready to make an effort to understand each other. And that will result in strong bonds of love and friendship.

So let us each begin exploring our relationship as allies carefully, ready to listen, and to defend each other against hurtful criticisms or misconceptions.

I was heartened, for example, to see that transmen and transwomen had created a workshop at this conference to deal with how to work with each other most sensitively. I have heard some non-trans people criticize transsexual women for taking up too much space or being too overbearing because they were socialized as males. It's one thing for transwomen to discuss issues of socialization as an internal discussion in transsexual space. But it's a prejudiced and dangerous formulation for non-transsexuals to make. It's a fast and slippery slide from the rigidity of biological determinism to an equally narrow position of social determinism.

And it too closely parallels transphobic attacks that charge: "Once a man, always a man; once a woman, always a woman." This line of reasoning flies in the face of the fact that consciousness is determined by *being*. When a man or woman comes out as gay, lesbian, or bisexual, they become part of those communities. No one says "once a heterosexual, always a heterosexual." The consciousness of lesbian, gay, and bisexual people changes and develops while living through the oppression, and working with others to fight back. That is true for transwomen, as well.

I am very wary of labeling people's energy as "male" or "female." The infinite and ever-changing ways people express themselves cannot be partitioned into two narrow categories. It's hazardous to gender the "energy" that people exude. For instance, Ashkenazi Jewish women have faced the anti-Semitic charge that they are guilty of exhibiting "male energy" because of what some non-Jews considered to be aggressive or loud behavior.

There are many factors that determine social behavior and interaction. And people interact differently as they work with many kinds of people. Those of us who grew up very isolated from other people began a process of socialization as we worked in coalitions over the years. We learned important communication skills. All of us came into movements with rough edges. Some raised their hands too often or dominated discussions, others interrupted speakers who had the floor. Those who had been in the movements for some time helped set guidelines and modify inappropriate behavior. Trans activists and organizers new to the movement have had little, if any, of that experience. Yet each person's contributions are valuable and deserve time to fully develop. Some of us have learned important lessons from some very harsh, angry people. I think most of us are grateful for the gently patient and compassionate lessons. That may offer us the best model for helping each other adapt to collective work. So let all of us who are not transsexual do everything possible to support transwomen and transmen.

In turn, the ways transsexual women and men characterize our movement can help build a wider basis for unity. I have heard the formulation that "transmen are half of the transgender community." But that's not true. Transmen are half of the *transsexual* community. Saying that transsexual men are half of the trans population, and transsexual women are the other half, considerably narrows the scope of our movement. It leaves out everyone who is not transsexual.

What about intersexual activists? What about the gay drag queens and kings who fought against police brutality at Stonewall? It leaves out masculine women and feminine men, cross-dressers, bi-genders, tri-genders, transgenderists, shape-shifters, morphers, bearded females – and many others.

I have heard an argument that transgender people oppress transsexual people because we are trying to tear down the categories of male and female. But isn't this the same reactionary argument used against transmen and transwomen by those who argue that any challenges to assigned birth sex threaten the categories of man and woman? Transgender people are not dismantling the categories of man and woman. We are opening up a world of possibilities in addition. Each of us has a right to our identities. To claim one group of downtrodden people is oppressing another by their self-identification is to swing your guns away from those who really do oppress us, and to aim them at those who are already under siege.

I remember a middle-class, predominantly white current of the early women's movement that opposed lesbian inclusion. They argued that strong, assertive women were already being lesbian-baited, so lesbian inclusion would just reinforce those attacks. But lesbians brought new strength to the women's movement, demonstrated the sexual diversity among women, and welded a more powerful coalition of allies against the oppression of all women, including lesbians.

There was a similar middle-class, white current in the early gay and lesbian movement that argued the media shouldn't show drag queens at Pride events because gay men and lesbians were already being gender-baited – told that they were not real men and women. But those who said "Don't take pictures of the drag queens, we're not all like that," weakened the movement they themselves depended on for liberation.

That doesn't mean we all have to forge one common self-definition. It means we support the right of each person to define themselves and we don't put down anyone else's identity. Sometimes individuals may not even realize they are putting someone else down. For example, a young transman told me recently, "I'm not like you drag kings. My identity is about more than just what clothes I wear."

Reducing the identities of drag queens and drag kings to the clothing we wear is insulting. We are *transgendered* people. We are in danger wherever we go because of our gender expression. And we have a long, proud history of fighting back.

Confusing our gender expression with our sexuality denies the reality of our battles as transgender people. For instance, the dismissal of butch females as "just lesbians" does injury to a very oppressed segment of our trans population. To start with, the "just" in that formulation is anti-lesbian. And what does the statement mean? Are all lesbians masculine? Do all lesbians face arrest or violence if they use women's restrooms? Is masculinity in women who desire other women just a sexual advertisement?

I prefer using the term *masculine female* instead of butch, because butch is assumed to mean lesbian. But what about masculine females who are bisexual? What about those who are heterosexual, some married to men who were attracted to them *because* of their masculinity, not in spite of it?

Aren't transmen similarly insulted by those who try to dismiss their manhood by arguing that they are "just lesbians" who couldn't deal with the oppression? Don't we all have a stake in refusing to let our sex or our gender expression be confused with our sexual desire?

The accusation that masculine females are not "real men" is also a familiar attack. But it's never succeeded in pushing us out of sight. We have always faced the charge that we are trying to be men and that we have failed miserably. But the muscles and sweat of masculine females helped accelerate the gains of the U.S. trade union movement—in heavy and light industry—particularly from the start of World War II to the end of the war against Vietnam. Today, with the shift to non-union, service industry jobs, we are fighting a battle to survive economically and socially.

We are not trying to be "real men." We are fighting to survive as masculine females. We face experiences that are differently complicated than those of women or men who are not transgendered. Those experiences develop our lives and our consciousness. And together with transgender males of all sexualities, we are a numerically huge segment of the trans population.

What is the bedrock on which all of our diverse trans populations can build solidarity? The commitment to be the best fighters against each other's oppression. As our activist network grows into marches and rallies of hundreds of thousands, we will hammer out language that demonstrates the sum total of our movement as well as its component communities.

Unity depends on respect for diversity, no matter what tools of language are ultimately used. This is a very early stage for trans peoples with such diverse histories and blends of cultures to form community. Perhaps we don't have to strive to be one community. In reality, there isn't one women's, or lesbian, gay, bi community. What is realistic is the goal to build a coalition between our many strong communities in order to form a movement capable of defending all our lives.

Movements are waves of people demanding redress of their grievances, crashing against those who profit from maintaining the status quo. Which political current will lead this movement? Like white-capped coastal rivers, movements are driven by many political currents. Which currents determine the course of the river for a time is also affected by external factors, like prevailing winds, storms, the inexorable pull of the moon and the resulting tides. And then there are the political storms ruling classes whip up to deflect mass protest—like scapegoating gay and bisexual men and Haitians for the spread of AIDS, or demonizing undocumented immigrant workers and people on welfare. The tides of mass popular reaction to these tempests – good or bad – affect the predominance of some movement currents over others. So do economic cycles – boom or bust – and the storms of bloody territorial wars between capitalist powers, like World War I and II.

So who will lead our movements today? Recently, many in the trans communities have been discussing "What makes a leader?" We've grown up in a society that places much more value on some human lives than on others, where a few are considered shepherds, and the rest sheep. We have been taught that we have no power to change the most miserable conditions of our lives. But that's a lie.

Everyone in this room is a leader. Each of us is needed as an organizer, as an activist in the decisive struggles that lie ahead.

There's a wonderful Chinese proverb that advises "The person who says it cannot be done should not interrupt the person doing it." The people who are making history today are the organizers, the activists, those who are building coalitions, distributing leaflets, making calls, sending out e-mail, mobilizing others out of their despair and into motion. The leaders are the ones who are "doing it." And the responsibility and role of leadership is to develop leadership in others.

In the words of African-American poet June Jordan, "We are the ones we have been waiting for."

I'm a gay transman of Apache and Scotch-Irish descent, left-handed, differently abled, the parent of two young children – one of whom is also differently abled – of an old Cracker frontier family from Texas, a person who values his Native heritage very deeply, and who is doing his best to live in accordance with the Spirit, and who keeps learning more about his heritage all the time. I am also the founder and Coordinator-in-Chief of the American Boyz, the largest grassroots f2m organization in North America with affiliates in twenty-three states and provinces, and for two years running now, the Chair of the True Spirit Conference for f2ms. I am also a gay author and editor, with several books in print, as well as numerous short stories.

Arriving at this current place has been a journey not only of self-discovery, but of discovery about my family and my culture. Coming out transgendered was easy; grappling with racism, classism and ableism and other barriers is much harder. Once I figured out that "transgendered" was someone who transcended traditional stereotypes of "man" and "woman," I saw that I was such a person. I then began a quest for finding words that described myself, and discovered that while psychiatric jargon dominated the discourse, there were many other words, both older and newer, that addressed these issues. While I accepted the label of "transsexual" in order to obtain access to the hormones and chest surgery necessary to manifest my spirit in the material world, I have always had a profound disagreement with the definition of transsexualism as a psychiatric condition and transsexuals as disordered people.

My own transgendered state is a sacred calling given to me by Spirit, not a neurosis discovered by white medicine. Further, the battles that rage in feminist circles and elsewhere about the legitimacy and nature of the transgendered identity smack of racism to me, centered as they are upon white experience and white authors to the exclusion of minority voices and viewpoints, many of which contradict some of the conventional wisdom about what transsexualism is and what it means. It is extremely important to remember that "transsexual" and "transgendered" are terms that have arisen out of the dominant culture's experience with gender, and are not necessarily reflective of a wide variety of people, cultures, beliefs, and practices relating to gender.

As a person of Native descent I look to my ancestors for guidance in these matters. But the record is broken; trying to learn about the sacred people is like trying to reassemble a million pieces of pottery with only a few hundred potshards as clues. This then is the thing I know: that Spirit gives to each of us Visions of who we are which we must manifest in the material world to the best of our ability. Transgendered people, combining elements of male and female, are at the interstice of the material and spiritual worlds and are thus able to act as mediators for the benefit of our communities. We earn honor for our wisdom and strength, measured by our hard work on behalf of our families and communities. For this reason the sacred people are an integral part of our communities, not alienated or shameful, but often hidden to protect them from the ravages of the dominant culture. And, where white culture has triumphed, they have been almost entirely lost to the contemporary Native world – which means that there are many Native people today who do not know about or who do not value our sacred people.

It is important for Native people to reclaim our sacred people who have been murdered, burned, beaten, hanged, imprisoned, flogged, stripped, humiliated, and otherwise forced into compliance with the dominant standards of gender and sexuality or exterminated when they resisted. It is common for white people to refer to these people as "berdache" if they have male genitalia, and as "amazons" if they have female genitalia, but these terms are offensive, being foreign terms that depend upon white standards of reference and which ignore Native traditions. I prefer to use the Sioux word "winkte" for those people who are described in English as "m2f" (male to female) and "kurami" (from the Yuma kwe'rhame) for people who are "f2m" (female to male). However, while these Native terms overlap in meaning with terminology used by the dominant society, they are not identical because Native concepts of gender and identity differ in significant ways from the dominant culture.

I don't use the term "two-spirit" to describe myself; where I grew up it was a pejorative term for a person of mixed blood. Further, there is no consensus of opinion as to just who is meant by the term "two-spirit," and not only that, if translated into Native tongues it acquires unfortunate meanings; among my people it means "ghost-haunted" – a powerful concept and important in many Native spiritual systems, but having nothing to do with gender or orientation.

In my understanding of Spirit, Spirit is not divided in itself, but is an integrated whole. It is not a thing in balance, as implied by dichotomies of male/female, gay/straight, and black/white so prevalent in the white way of thinking; but a complete and complex thing which includes an entire rainbow of possibilities – not just the opposite ends of a spectrum. That is why there are seven cardinal directions: east, west, north, south, up, down, and center, as the Native viewpoint embraces dimensions not normally noticed by the dominant culture; so too does Spirit embrace dimensions of humanity not normally accepted by the dominant culture. There are many names for sexual minorities among Native Americans; two-spirits are a particular community that have elected that term to describe themselves, but I am not one of them.

There are many "magpies" who are drawn to latch onto the bright, shiny aspects of Native culture, who misappropriate Native culture, customs, and artifacts in the belief that they are "honoring" Native people by imitating them without understanding them. It is better for non-Native people to follow our example by looking to their own ancestors and reclaiming their own transgendered spirituality. European cultures from the Vikings to the Greeks had and honored transgendered people; even the Christian Church recognized saints that lived as members of the opposite sex or engaged in same sex unions. No European culture lacks a transgendered tradition; white people need to reclaim their own sacred people instead of appropriating ours.

The process of reclamation is an extraordinarily difficult one in which the seeker must come face to face with the atrocities of the past, grieve for what has been lost, and carefully sift through the destruction to recover the little that remains. This is true whether the seeker is examining Native American or Euro-American history. History is not ancient and irrelevant; history is the reason why things are the way they are now.

GARY BOWEN IS A GAY AUTHOR, EDITOR, COWBOY AND A MEMBER OF THE
WESTERN WRITERS ASSOCIATION (WWA) AND INTERNATIONAL GAY
RODEO ASSOCIATION (IGRA). E-MAIL: FCOWBOY@NETGSI.COM (THE FLYING COWBOY).
URL: HTTP://WWW.NETGSI.COM/~FCOWBOY (HIGH PLAINS DRIFTER OF
THE INTERNET)

4.

*O*n the tense moments before the
True Spirit Conference workshop
titled "Exploring Our Options" began, the
fear and pain in the room was palpable. I know, because I felt it all churn-
ing in the pit of my stomach, as well. An organized discussion on this
subject, on such a large scale, had never really taken place, to my knowledge. Woman or man. Feminine female or masculine male. What if you
couldn't – or wouldn't – squeeze your body and spirit into those categories, or loved someone who couldn't or wouldn't? How would you
define yourself? What combination of words could approximate your
identity? How much courage would it take to try to describe your identity, perhaps for the first time, to a roomful of strangers?

I sat on a panel with two other trans people. Each of us opened with
our ideas about the workshop, and a brief description of our own lives and
identities. And then, for almost two hours, individuals in the workshop
began to speak. What happened in the course of that discussion was life
changing for many of us. I've never been in a room in which this particular pain was articulated so sharply. And I've never felt as joyful or as hope-
ful in a room filled with people I'd never met before, either. The laughter
in that workshop was the kind that washes you clean from the inside out.
And the collectively shed tears released a flood of rage and shame.

I want so much for you to hear every word that was spoken in that workshop, to sit through every long silence we shared. But I respect the confidentiality in that room. The world is a dangerous place for each of us as trans people — no matter where we find ourselves on the arcs of sex and gender. So in order for you to hear all our voices, we need you to help us create a place to talk that is as safe as that workshop was. I believe you will.

In the meantime, here are my remarks from that discussion.

This is a workshop that took courage to attend. It is a workshop for those of us who sit in front of an application trying to figure out which of two boxes to check off — "F" or "M" — neither of which exactly fits our lives and our self-identities. You could write down "not applicable" or "none of the above" or "all of the above" next to those two little boxes, but it won't get you a job. It won't get you a driver's license. It won't get you a passport.

Because it is legally mandated that all our lives must fit into one of those two tiny boxes, many of us actually face imprisonment or institutionalization merely because we don't. We live under the constant threat of horrifying violence. We have to worry about what bathroom to use when our bladders are aching. We are forced to consider whether we'll be dragged out of a bathroom and arrested or face a fistfight while our bladders are still aching. It's an everyday reality for us. Human beings must use toilets.

This is a workshop for those of us who grapple with this simple, yet humiliating question every day: If I go into the women's bathroom, am I prepared for the shouting and shaming? Will someone call security or the cops? If I use the men's room, am I willing to fight my way out? Am I really ready for the violence that could ensue? And how can I protect my humanity – my very being – from the degradation of having to make these decisions several times a day? No one ever taught us how to deal with the question of public toilets.

Many of us have identities that we have no language for. "Are you a guy, or what?" We are the anvils, and that question hammers us daily. For us, the question requires more than a one-word answer.

It seems as though everyone who questions the totality of who we are – whether they despise us or admire us – thinks that an answer to the question "Are you a woman or a man?" will illuminate our identities. But for some of us in this room, the ground we have staked out in the space between those two poles is precious. There is no one word at this time that will put the question of our identities to rest.

All of us here have fought to defend our right to complexity in a society that demands we compress the totality of being into *feminine* woman. Unless that category is a comfortable choice, it becomes a suffocating compartment.

Many of us can't fit these sex/gender definitions; others of us don't want to fit. As alluring as the notion of "belonging" can be on a hard day, we don't want to give up the basis of our insights, of our consciousness, of what we want to bring to other human beings in interaction and how we want to be interacted with.

I will tell you a little about my own identity as a trans person. What makes me transgendered is that my birth sex – which is female – appears to be in social contradiction to my gender expression – which is read as masculine. I defend my right to that social contradiction. In fact, I want to live long enough to hear people ask, "What made me think that was a contradiction in the first place?"

It's true that in this society, at this point in time, being a masculine female seems as though it is a contradiction, and so I am forced to try to find language to explain myself. But in ancient cooperative societies all over the world, someone whose gender was similar to mine would be respected. Knowing that historical truth helps me hold my head up high.

I live proudly in a body of my own design.

I defend my right to be complex.

I am a person who does not wish to be referred to as Ms. or Mr.

I respect the right of each person who finds their home in man or woman, male or female, to refer to themselves as Ms. or Mr., she or he. And I appreciate the anti-sexist struggle that was waged to create the address "Ms." When I was growing up, the question "Is that Miss or Mrs.?" seemed to be coded into all human interchanges. I didn't think that automatic conversational response could be rooted out. Yet in just a few short decades I've seen Ms. come into popular usage. I think that's because the question "Miss or Mrs.?" was inherently offensive. The root of the query was: Are you somebody's property or are you still on the loose? So bringing Ms. into usage was progressive.

I think it's equally progressive to open up a wider discussion about the offensive social attitudes built into the limitation of English language pronouns. If we hear someone described to us who we've never met, we've already unconsciously made assumptions about that person based on the pronoun used to describe them. And one of the biggest assumptions built into the pronouns is that the person must be one or the other. That's where the pronoun "it" comes in. That pronoun is hurled at those of us who don't appear to fit *he* or *she*. The gender-neutral pronoun "it" is an epithet meant to strip us of our humanity. We need a gender-neutral pronoun that honors us as unique human beings.

I personally prefer gender-neutral pronouns. I don't expect everyone to begin using them overnight. But I see, particularly in cyberspace, that these pronouns seem to be coming into usage relatively quickly.

And so we should feel free to use alternative or gender-neutral pronouns during this workshop. Some people use either *s/he* or *sie* – both pronounced "sea," like the ocean. Others use *ze* (zee). The possessive gender-neutral pronoun coming into popular usage is *hir* (like here and now). It is easier for some people, at first, to use these pronouns in writing than in speech because we've been so conditioned all our lives to use *she* or *he*.

I asked Beacon Press to use *s/he* in the author description of me on the cover of *Transgender Warriors*. That pronoun is a contribution from the women's liberation movement. Prior to that struggle, the pronoun "he" was almost universally used to describe humankind –"mankind." So *s/he* opened up the pronoun to include "womankind." I used *s/he* on my book jacket because it is recognizable as a gender-neutral pronoun to people.

But I personally prefer the pronoun *ze* because, for me, it melds mankind and womankind into humankind.

Too many of us as trans people have experienced something similar to the "Miss or Mrs." query – except it feels much more demeaning. It's the address I call "Mamsir." You know what I mean: "Here's your change ma'am, I mean sir, I mean ma'am, I mean sir." It's debasing and embarrasses both people and anyone else who is listening. I despise the class subordination that resides in those once mandatory forms of address, as well.

On a good day, when I have the strength, I say to the clerk "Wouldn't it be easier to just say: Here's your change; have a nice day"?

To me, that's what this workshop is all about. How can we define ourselves in ways that honor our self-expression – our very beings? Let us try. There are no hostile observers here. There is no one who will humiliate you or criticize you for the words you sort through and try on to describe yourself.

And as you struggle to identify yourself in words, you offer every one of us here the gift of new language – of fresh concepts. It really is your contribution to us. You do not have to bare your soul – or you can. You can talk about yourself in the third person. Do whatever is most comfortable for you.

Our discussion here today will eventually help change the way people think about what's "natural" and "normal." We are representative of the expanse of human variance, yet we do not see ourselves in culture, in language, or in everyday life, except in very twisted and distorted ways. This is a chance to represent our own lives in our own words.

The knowledge that we are in a workshop that is going to help reshape the consciousness of future generations is not meant to be a responsibility that keeps any of us silent. Just the opposite. Let that knowledge soften the clenched muscles of our jaws. Each of our truths, articulated, is eloquent.

From looking around at the emotions etched on the faces I see in this room, I know that we will all make sure this is a safe space for you to speak. All of us here have been terribly hurt. One workshop will not heal all injuries that we've experienced, nor will it completely prepare us for what lies ahead between this True Spirit Conference and the next.

In my opinion, we need on-going discussion groups and Internet bulletin boards and other means of communication that allow us to continue speaking to each other. We need to know when we are alone that we will soon be coming together again, in even larger numbers.

Today we have found each other. And from now on, we never again feel as alone as we've felt our entire lives. This is a very important moment for all of us. It's been a long, arduous journey. But we found each other.

You are home now.

MICHAEL HERNANDEZ

"I am neither man nor woman"

We are told from the time that we learn to walk that the magic number is two: male/female, black/white, right/wrong, day/night, sun/moon, good/evil . . . the list goes on and on. People seem to casually ignore the fact that there are more than two races, an entire field has been dedicated to the gray area between right and wrong (i.e. Ethics), dawn and dusk separate night and day, an entire universe of planets, stars, wormholes, and more exist, and good and evil depend largely on religion and/or perspective. Yet two remains the battle cry until we get to behavior and then the magic number is one. We are told that there is only one way to be, one way to act, one way to feel.

The One True Path dictates that all people are alike and should want the same things. That those who are different are to be converted at the earliest possible opportunity. Those who fail or refuse to convert are to be ostracized or better yet, killed, for fear that they will taint the true followers.

The One True Path conscripts people into marriage and buying that house with the white picket fence further mandating that all people be heterosexual and that they procreate, but only after marriage. That there is only One God and you better toe the line or else.

I broke away from the One True Path when I came out as a lesbian. I was exhilarated to be free from the oppressive gender coded rules. I broke away from that when I walked on the fringe of that community and again was exhilarated for a time before finding that each community that I have been a part of has its own rules and ideology.

When I first started taking testosterone, I believed in two as the magic number. After a number of years as the invisible man, it was impossible for me not to overcompensate. I needed to belong somewhere and I was convinced that belonging was being like-minded. Like-minded has become tainted for me. It is full of dogma and exclusion and an exorcism of that which is different. Time passed and experience colored my perceptions of the world. As I grew more comfortable with myself I found a balance, a sense of peace. I am more than male and more than female. I am neither man nor woman, but the circle encompassing both.

My lesbian culture and heritage are important and as the days pass it is the female side that disappears from view yet colors my opinions, actions, and belief system. I am now perceived as the privileged white male despite the fact that there is less legal protection for transpeople and I can be fired or not hired for my gender status. I'm Latino, and my body remains a mixture of secondary female and male characteristics. No one rides for free.

It is difficult enough being transgendered without throwing sexual orientation into the mix. I am on the fringe of society by being transgendered, on the fringe of the transgendered community by being homosexual and on the fringe of that community by being transgendered. Would that be considered fringe cubed? What about my identity as both lesbian and gay? What happens when leather gets thrown into the mix? The mathematics boggle the mind.

In struggling with who I am and where I belonged, I learned that there was no consensus from the outside. Everybody had a different opinion. Only I had the answers to these questions and they were certainly not taken as valid by everyone. Yet only I can live my life and decide what is right for me. If I rely on someone else to make these decisions or set policy for me, then I am destined for disappointment.

I just am. The name and the fit aren't that important anymore. There is always something that will make me different. It's a part of my nature and a part of my path. I have grown beyond the numbers game.

There are more than two or even three. Gender and behavior are as variable as the stars in the sky. There is no typical pattern which provides definitive proof that one is transgendered. There are so many similarities and even exact childhood histories in those who identify as lesbian, transsexual, or transgendered, that it is impossible to rely on someone else's experience to define yourself. No one has the answer, but you, and that answer is subject to change without notice.

My life today is very different than yesterday. There are days when I know where I am going and days where the doubts overwhelm. All in all I am a better person because I found my own way in the world. It may not be the same as yours and it certainly is not better than yours, but it is the right way for me.

*"The man and the little
girl within have finally
joined hands"*

I moved out to the Pacific Northwest and fell in
love with the sky. Perhaps it is the dampness of
my Irish heritage that makes me love it so. But more I think it is the thousand shades of grey that the sky is – you look above you and there are such infinite possibilities.

I've lived parts of my life as a straight woman, as a butch dyke, as a man – both straight and faggot. Each was and is important. I'm not about to forget anything if I can help it, but rather walk the circle as I see it. I think, as I get older, I become stranger and more generic. A generic queer, for queer is my nation and my culture.

I had the chest surgery last spring (1997) after many years of binding my chest to look male but not having the "lop 'em offa me." Don't know exactly why I waited so long, for it has been very freeing to me to do this. The best part of it was something I did not expect. It is as though the man and the little girl within have finally joined hands in alliance and love – much love! They both have a flat chest, you see. It is so good to have her back again and strong again in me.

I think of myself as man and woman, both and neither these days. The world out there sometimes wonders out loud at me. There are a few practical details that sometimes present a challenge. But on the whole, I like being on the bridge. And even when I am having trouble with it that day, I know it's where I belong. That's good – knowing that. You can write the rules for yourself, and change them. You can walk in this world, harming no one. There really is room for everyone to be. People are sometimes afraid of me and I hope to calm their fear. The only way for sure to kill the fear that someone may walk through your walls is to knock your walls down.

I love the word "transition." Everybody's always in transition, so we really all have a lot in common.

My son, now age 17, is the best. I thank him for so much. I was flying scared, by the seat of my pants when he was born, and now I fly with skill and care.

S/M and ritual are a part of my life. I think it's so important to see the beauty that grows in spite of the pain and destruction in the world. Just look at the blades of grass that grow in the cracks of the concrete in the middle of the highway. That's a ritual, all by itself.

5.

Ironically, the morning I arrived at the Boston Convention Center to speak to the 2nd Transgender Health Conference, I felt sick as a dog. As I climbed the steps to the stage, I wasn't sure I'd be able to stand and speak. From the podium, I could see about 350 people, filling the auditorium. I knew some worked at AIDS service centers; others were health care providers. Some were gay, lesbian, and bi; others were heterosexual; a few were trans. Some were assigned by their agencies to attend; others came on their own accord.

I felt so ill the room seemed to spin. Yet if I stepped down from this podium, where would I go to seek health care? I decided to attempt to speak, and if I couldn't continue, I'd ask for help from the audience.

I'm very lucky to be alive today and able to speak to you about the health care crisis for trans people. I hovered near death all last year – unable to secure a diagnosis, tests, or a cure. Two obstacles blocked my path like boulders: bigotry and poverty. Both are deadly roadblocks in an economic system that organizes health care as a profit-driven industry.

When my fever first spiked, I did not have a doctor to call. As a transgender adult, I had only sought treatment in life-and-death situations. Moments when I was weakened and scared because of illness were times I least relished a stranger examining my body; I felt vulnerable to potential hostility.

I remembered the resident who, while examining me for strep throat, suddenly shoved his hand down my pants, shouting, "You're a freak!"

I remembered the doctor who told me in a quiet voice that the devil — not Jesus — had encouraged me to choose the path I've walked in life.

I remembered every moment of humiliation I'd ever experienced at the hands of health care providers. That's why I always made up a phony nom de guerre and gave bogus ID to emergency room staff. Get out with a quick medical evaluation, a prescription and my dignity — that was always my aim.

Of course that meant I'd never had any continuity of care from a primary physician who I could trust to treat my body with caring and respect. Instead I'd had to grapple with the fear that the malice or contempt of the doctor or nurse would result in poor or malicious mistreatment.

Unfortunately, this is not an individual crisis. Throughout the United States, masculine females and feminine males, crossdressers, transsexuals and intersexuals are home alone dealing with pain, fevers, the trauma of gang rape and beatings, and other emergencies, hoping the symptoms will go away so they don't have to reveal themselves to a venomously hostile doctor or nurse.

In 1995 my symptoms did not go away. I was incubating a deadly bacterial heart infection, and as a result, I developed acute cytomegalovirus and other diseases.

Like tens of millions of documented workers in this country, and uncounted millions of undocumented workers, I had no health insurance. Paying the rent and buying food has always been a struggle for me. As a visibly transgendered person I have always had low-wage jobs, if any. I had no savings or pension fund to dip into. And in fact, no working person can afford a catastrophic illness, even if they save a small nest egg.

So with a raging fever I made my way on the subway, through a sleet storm, to a clinic that has a sliding payment scale. The waiting area was standing room only. Young mothers held a crying infant in one arm and clutched a restless toddler's hand with another. Elderly people sat alone; they leaned their heads back against the wall, or they doubled over coughing.

The staff was sometimes rude to us. But they were just as abrupt with each other. Five hours later, as I still sat waiting to be seen, I had a better sense of how overworked they were.

In fact, the staff was so overburdened that the clinic was nearly dysfunctional. The results of my blood test were misplaced. Had they not been lost, I could have been cured after eight weeks of intravenous treatment. This was just the first of the tragedy of errors and hurdles to health care that resulted in a year of grave illness, needless intravenous medications, discrimination, abuse, powerlessness, and rage.

You see, I could be like a transgender Scheherazade. I could tell you horror stories about how I and other trans people have been treated by the health care system from now to my last breath and there'd still be more outrages to relate.

You might feel such seething rage at health care workers that you would stand up with us as trans people *against* them. But that's not my goal. I want you to be angry about the abuses we have suffered.

I want you to help us create zero tolerance for gender-phobia and trans-phobia in the health care industry. But I believe that pitting patients against health care staff only exacerbates the problem. The only way we can begin to create change in the care of trans people is to open up a dialogue with health care workers.

But there are obstacles that prevent such a discussion from taking place. Bigotry is pandemic in this society, so the education of health care workers has to be part of our larger struggle to build alliances between everyone who suffers from discrimination and prejudice.

The owners and CEOs of the lucrative health care industry try to block a large-scale dialogue from developing between staff and patients, as well. For example, I can't name the doctor who told me my fever was a result of my being "a very troubled person." I can't name the hospital in which I awoke at night to find staff gawking at me, laughing and referring to me as "it." I can't name the staff who referred to me as a Martian.

If I did, the hospital administrators, on behalf of the owners, could sue me. Is this litigation threat meant to protect hospital workers? No, the threats of libel suits are designed to protect the hospital corporations from financial damages.

We as trans people have no interest in hurting health care workers. We have a stake in building camaraderie between us. We can offer important feedback on how the administration of health care is structured in ways that create a schism between trans patients and health care workers. For example, the hospital into which I was admitted mandated that patients be placed in wards based on birth biology. That meant that I was placed on a female ward, where my masculinity created an immediate furor. This same hospital places male-to-female transsexual women who have completed sex-reassignment surgery on male wards. In which ward will intersexual people fit?

Some might argue that this is a division based on nature. I heard similar arguments used to defend racial segregation in health care services when I was a child. Racial segregation wasn't decreed by nature; it was rooted in racism. Trans oppression is not identical to racist oppression. But prejudice and hatred nearly killed me because I didn't fit into the rigid female or male ward system.

Wouldn't it make sense to create wards based on the type of injury or disease and the degree of care required? Many hospitals place females and males in separate rooms within mixed wards without dire consequence. In such a situation, the patient's gender expression or sex creates much less of a stir.

And we have a right to demand that health care institutions provide mandatory sensitivity classes in which representatives from diverse trans communities can have an opportunity to speak to the staff.

Some nurses and physician's assistants and doctors will hear us and quickly understand that trans people deserve to be treated with respect. But I say to those who hold opinions about transgender and intersexuality and transsexuality that they're not willing to let go of: If you feel you can't treat us compassionately then do us both a favor — remove yourself from the situation. Let us work with someone on the staff who is sensitive to our humanity.

Even well-intentioned health care providers can be hampered in their approach to trans patients based on what they've been taught is natural. A very caring nurse recently told me she wished trans people would inform her of that fact right away. If she finds out later, she feels duped. And she believes it's important for their care that she knows what their birth biology is.

To be blunt, it's really not her business. Each trans patient must have the fundamental right to privacy. The question of patient self-revelation can't be seen solely through a clinical lens. There are larger social issues. Maybe you feel you would treat this patient the same way once they came out to you. But when you put it in their chart, or mention it to the next staff member, the trans patient may be mistreated.

Underlying the anger or embarrassment of health care workers who feel "tricked" by a trans patient is the feeling that "I thought you were one sex, but you're *really* another." You're really another. What does that mean? That trans people are pretending to be something that they're not?

This view is based on biological determinism – a weapon used for centuries to justify the oppression of women. Biological determinism only regards the sex we are assigned at birth as authentic.

All of our lives and our identities are valid and real. But if we don't come out to health care personnel, it's not because we are duplicitous. It's because we are oppressed.

Winning more sensitive care for trans people is not enough to save our lives. Not if we can't afford to see a doctor or go to a hospital. The fight against bigotry must go hand in hand with the battle to make health care affordable.

And in this fight, trans people do not stand alone.

Today we are witnessing the final stages of the transfer of health care to an industry run solely to make profits. The changes in health care parallel those now occurring in all large businesses and financial institutions. Smaller hospitals and health care facilities are consolidating into large-scale corporations. Hospitals are closing their doors in communities that desperately need them because the facilities are deemed unprofitable. Public health centers are being privatized. Profits are being maximized by downsizing the number of workers and speeding up those still employed.

Patients' lives are held hostage to the greed of the pharmaceutical giants that patent drugs used to treat life-threatening diseases. When I contracted acute cytomegalovirus during a catastrophic illness last year, the cost for one month's medication was out of reach for me: $13,000. With government deregulation, private insurance companies pick and choose those they feel are healthy, and reject disabled, ill, and elderly people.

Medical science can achieve microsurgical organ transplants, gene manipulation and splicing. In this epoch of rapidly expanding medical knowledge, why is a treatable disease like tuberculosis again on the rise amongst the poor in this country? Why are more and more people being shunted into HMOs where treatment cost is the bottom line? Why are Medicaid and Medicare being whittled away instead of expanded?

Because the productive growth under capitalism isn't designed to meet human needs. Each hospital, each insurance carrier, is only concerned with its own bottom line.

How can we wage a political battle to expand access to affordable, adequate, and sensitive health care? By fusing the power of the poorest and most oppressed communities, people with AIDS and their service providers, elders, the lesbian, gay, bi, and trans movements, civil rights organizations, the women's movement, and labor – employed and unemployed.

Together we can demand that the government channel the necessary funds to meet public health emergencies like AIDS and breast cancer. And that welfare, Medicaid, and Medicare assistance be restored and expanded to all who need it. We can demand that every patient be treated with respect, and that every vestige of prejudice must be eradicated from health care.

We can demand that every form of health care be free – from emergency to preventive care, from open-heart surgery to prenatal care, from eyeglasses to dentures, from lab work to drugs. Open the doors of medical schools to all who want an education and eliminate the staggering costs of tuition. We deserve free health care because it is a right, not a privilege.

Do you think that's a lot to ask for? That it sounds utopian? Well, my partner Minnie Bruce just returned from three weeks of working and living with families in Cuba – a tiny island of 11 million people burdened by the legacy of colonialism and being economically strangled by an illegal U.S. blockade. One of the many achievements of the Revolution that most impressed her was that every single person in Cuba receives free health care – from the womb to the tomb. And preventive care – not just emergency attention. Glasses, braces, surgery, prescriptions – all are free to everyone. Medical schools – all education – is free too, because education, like health care and a job, is considered the birthright of every human being.

The United States is the richest country in the world, we are often told.

So show us the money!

In fact, the greatest polarization of wealth and poverty in the world exists here in the United States. That's why it will take a *collective* fight to win the health care we deserve. Remember how Medicaid and Medicare were won in the first place? By people who got fed up waiting for the next election. They took to the streets to vote with their feet in picket lines and marches and sit-ins and rallies.

It will take just such a mighty movement to provide every human being with sensitive, respectful, and free health care.

Each of us deserves nothing less.

"Until five years ago, intersexuals remained silent"

At first, it seemed as if some karmic conjunction was working in my favor. In 1992, just when I had finally overcome my crippling shame and decided to speak out about being intersex and suffering a clitorectomy, the country was buzzing about genital mutilation. Alice Walker's book *Possessing the Secret of Joy* was a best-seller; editorials in staid mainstream media outlets decried clitorectomy as a violation of human rights, as child abuse, as barbarism. Surely, when they heard that mutilating genital surgeries were performed on a routine basis in American hospitals, the media would be all over the story, right?

Wrong. Now, five years later, with prominent coverage in *Newsweek*, the *New York Times*, the *San Francisco Chronicle*, and on NBC *Dateline*, the issue has finally hit the nation's radar. How was this accomplished? Why did it take as long as it did?

Since the late 1950s in the United States, it has been standard to treat the birth of a child with unusual genitals as a "social emergency," and to remedy the discomfort of parents and doctors by genital surgery on the infant. Motivated in part by a fear that the children might grow up homosexual, doctors perform cosmetic genital surgery on about 1 in 2,000 children. The vast majority medically unnecessary, these surgeries remove clitoral tissue, excavate vaginal cavities, or move or extend urethras. Outcomes are poor in functional, cosmetic, and emotional terms. Surgeries are often repeated, sometimes over a dozen times. A profound shame prevents people from discussing what has happened to them.

Denunciations of African surgeries serve as a sort of proxy. The none-too-subtle message is that Africans do not respect women, or that Africans are irrational and unscientific, or that Africans do not love and protect their children. Implied is that "we" (i.e. enlightened Americans) respect women, are rational and scientific, and love and protect our children.

What a contrast with our own medicalized genital surgeries. To examine this issue, we must confront the fact that one of the very establishments we hold dear does not always respect women (surgeons assign nine out of ten intersex infants they see as girls because "it's easier"), are not always rational (whatever doctors do is respected as "scientific," even when it makes little sense), and do not always love or protect our children (psychologist Suzanne Kessler notes that genital ambiguity is "corrected" because it threatens not the infant's life but the culture the infant is born into).

But we refused to be powerless, and a combination of persistence, self-education, and coalition led us to strategies which ultimately turned the tide.

Until five years ago, intersexuals remained silent, paralyzed by shame and each unaware that s/he was not alone. The history of the gay and lesbian movement shows that overcoming shame is crucial to forming a successful social movement. Following a 1993 article by Anne Fausto-Sterling on intersexuality, the magazine *The Sciences* published my letter announcing the formation of the Intersex Society of North America (ISNA). That letter, and a few others, brought correspondence from a handful of other intersexuals, all similarly emotionally traumatized and many surgically mutilated as well. We took immense comfort from finding others like ourselves, and from learning others had also experienced their "care" as a betrayal, as punishment for being different.

By late 1994 we collected some of our stories into the first issue of a newsletter called *Hermaphrodites with Attitude*, a venue in which our stories could be made public without sacrificing our privacy. The first issue of our newsletter inaugurated an ISNA tradition: humor. Rudolph the Red-Nosed Reindeer graced the cover, with a hand-colored red nose on each copy. The accompanying article satirized medical literature on intersex genital surgery by discussing Rudolph's nose as a disfiguring deformity, and an "after surgery" picture, captioned "excellent cosmetic result," depicted a clearly mutilated Rudolph in tears.

I wrote to many physicians who practice on intersex children and are respected as medical authorities. I urged them to consider that they were attempting to treat the very real pain of social stigma by erasing or hiding the stigmatized characteristic. Real healing will come only by decreasing the stigma, and that will come not from hiding, but from coming out, from asserting pride in who we are. My correspondence was almost universally ignored by doctors, which told me that change would be effected only by bringing the issue to wider social attention.

In part as a means of trying to generate media coverage, I cultivated interest and support within non-medical professional communities. By 1996 we had a large pool of sex researchers, psychologists, sociologists, psychotherapists, historians, ethicists, and psychiatrists who would tell journalists that physicians are simply missing the picture. The work of historian/ethicist Alice Dreger, feminist critic of science Anne Fausto-Sterling, and gender theorist Suzanne Kessler analyzed the process by which the medical mistreatment of intersexuals had come into being. This sort of historicizing is a powerful technique; it allows us to say, "It wasn't always that way, it got made that way. And if it got made that way, it can get unmade."

The growth of the Internet has been a great boon for us. We have been able to leverage our computer skills into high visibility, making it very easy for intersexuals, parents, journalists, and professionals to find us. Internet mailing lists have made it easy for us to bring our issues to professional communities outside the medical profession. It is not an over-statement to say that without the Internet, it would have taken decades to get where we are now.

Working in concert with more established queer activist groups, we were able to generate some credibility by mere association. The Gay and Lesbian Medical Association was supportive, carrying some of our releases in their newsletter, and inviting us to present a panel at their annual meeting in summer of 1996. The Association of Gay and Lesbian Psychiatrists helped us to set up a case presentation at the APA's annual meeting in spring 1997, with an associated open house. Perhaps even more significant than the education of a few dozen physicians that was accomplished at each of these events was the fact that the media took us more seriously, merely because we had gained a medical audience.

In September 1996, Congress passed Pat Schroeder's "Female Genital Mutilation" bill, which prohibited clitoral surgery – except the sort practiced on intersexuals. Schroeder ignored requests by ISNA and by Anne Fausto-Sterling to word the bill in such a way as to protect American children as well as immigrant daughters. In October an impromptu group calling themselves Hermaphrodites with Attitude picketed the annual pediatricians' convention in Boston.

By January of 1997, the intersex cause was beginning to win many doubters, and a few actual converts, among medical intersex specialists. We had a large community of adult intersexuals who had healed enough of their shame to be able to speak publicly; we had a few parents who were willing to speak about their experiences and could rebut doctors' assertions that "things are so much better now." We had sexologists, sociologists, psychotherapists, historians, and even one or two surgeons and ethicists on our side.

Just as all of these pieces fell into place, a stroke of good luck came to us. Sex researcher Milton Diamond publicized the real outcome of what has become known as the "John/Joan" story. In the early 1960s, one of identical male twins had his penis accidentally destroyed during a botched circumcision. Doctors decided that a boy without a penis was no boy, so they would remove his testes and have his parents raise him as a girl. Later, sexologist John Money reported that "John" had developed quite nicely into a woman named "Joan," and this single case was considered evidence that boys born with small penises could be made into girls. In March of this year, Diamond reported that John had come forward to say that he had never been comfortable as a girl, that as a teen he had refused additional "feminizing" genital surgeries and hormones, and that he was now once again living as a man.

Diamond's report turned into a huge media event, reported on the front page of the *New York Times* and other major papers, in the news weeklies, and permeating the rest of the media from there. Most of the coverage spun the story as a unique mishap whose principal interest lay in the evidence it provided that sex differences are innate. By doing so, many in the media painted feminists as working against Nature by asserting that certain gendered differences are social, not biological.

The daily victims of the same medical treatment are labeled "hermaphroditic" or "intersexual," making it hard to identify or sympathize with us: "Oh, it's a medical condition." But John was agreed to be a "normal" male, which allowed people to recognize his story as a tragedy. Indeed, the fact that he married a woman and adopted children raises the specter that the doctors who insisted he wear a skirt and date boys were attempting to turn him into a (gasp!) homosexual.

We took advantage of the press's attention to the John/Joan story, making them aware that intersex children are treated every day with the sorts of medical arrogance, mutilating surgery, and willful deception that were imposed on John.

The recent media coverage in *Newsweek,* the *New York Times,* and others has been very successful for us precisely because it presents the story as one of struggle and social justice (a story about us, our culture), rather than about *them* (intersexuals as freaks). But without a lot of help from our friends, we would never have gotten here.

Gays, lesbians, and bisexuals are stigmatized and oppressed because they violate social standards for acceptable sex behavior; transsexuals because they violate standards for sex identity. Intersexuals are punished for violating social standards of acceptable sex anatomy. But our oppressions stem from the same source: rigid cultural definitions of sex categories, whether in terms of behavior, identity, or anatomy. I plan to be part of a movement where we work together against that common source of oppression.

EXCERPTED, WITH CHERYL CHASE'S PERMISSION, FROM HER ARTICLE ENTITLED "MAKING MEDIA — AN INTERSEX PERSPECTIVE," WHICH APPEARED IN THE FALL 1997 ISSUE OF IMAGES MAGAZINE, PUBLISHED BY THE GAY AND LESBIAN ALLIANCE AGAINST DEFAMATION.

CHERYL CHASE IS THE EXECUTIVE DIRECTOR OF THE INTERSEX SOCIETY OF NORTH AMERICA, A PEER SUPPORT, EDUCATION, AND ADVOCACY GROUP FOUNDED AND OPERATED BY AND FOR INTERSEXUALS. CHASE CAN BE REACHED VIA: INTERSEX SOCIETY OF NORTH AMERICA, P.O. BOX 31791, SAN FRANCISCO, CA 94131; E-MAIL: INFO@ISNA.ORG; WEB SITE: HTTP://WWW.ISNA.ORG

6.

*At 8 A.M. on a chilly spring Sunday morn-
ing I got into a van with four lesbians I'd
never met before. They had driven a long
way in order to make it easy for me to get to a conference of regional
Pride Committees, meeting in a hotel in Central New Jersey. As we
headed toward the Turnpike, they explained that I would be speaking
to activists who organize lesbian, gay, and bisexual Pride marches and
rallies from Maine to Washington, D.C. Some of those Pride committees, like the New Jersey group, already included* transgender *or* trans
*in the title of their events. My goal was to inspire other committees to
do likewise.*

*When we arrived at the hotel, the halls were crowded with activists
engaged in animated conversations. I found the conference room and
left a leaflet about an upcoming protest against federal budget cuts
and repression on each chair. As people filed into the room and sat
down, I watched them read the flyer. I understood that I was in a room
with seasoned grass-roots organizers. First, people read the text and
demands. Then many concentrated on the list of endorsing individuals and groups. I watched people delightedly point out endorsers to
each other.*

I knew these were people whose lives were much like mine — spent writ-

ing leaflets and press releases, making phone calls, sending e-mail, seal-
ing envelopes, forging pride, fighting back. I believed that if I could
explain why the inclusion of trans people would enhance that struggle,
many in this room would move heaven and earth to build the coalition. I
had written a talk, but the feeling in the room was so intimate that I was
concerned about sounding like I was "speechifying." So I put away my
prepared remarks and spoke from my heart.

I believe that the liberation of lesbians, gays, bisexuals, and trans people cannot be won without fighting back shoulder to shoulder.

In my life, these struggles are inseparable. I am oppressed because of my sexual desire, and I am oppressed because of my gender expression. I came out as a teenager into the blue-collar, pre-Stonewall gay drag bars of upstate New York and southern Ontario. We fought fierce battles that paved the way for the early gay liberation movement to march into the streets.

Did we fight back because our love was outlawed? Or because we were gender outlaws? I never thought to ask myself that question. I don't remember any of my friends ever formulating that question. We closed ranks and fought hard.

But just because I never stopped to ponder the question doesn't mean it isn't an important one to answer, because it clarifies the relationship between our communities. For example, African-American and Latina drag queens were on the front lines of the four-nights-running uprising against police brutality in Greenwich Village in 1969 that ignited the gay liberation movement. So was Stonewall a gay or a trans insurrection?

I recently put that question to Puerto Rican drag queen Sylvia Rivera – a combatant at Stonewall. I asked her, "Were you fighting police brutality? Were you fighting racism? Or for your right to be gay? Did you fight because so few of the queens could produce the military draft cards government agents demanded that night? Or because so many of you were homeless and hungry and embattled on the streets?"

Sylvia replied with quiet dignity, "We were fighting for our lives."

Was Stonewall a high-water mark in the battle for gay or trans liberation?

Sylvia offers us the most succinct, eloquent answer possible: It was both. The oppressions overlap in the lives of gay drag people. Mixed in the blood we shed when we fight back are all the elements of who we are.

Yet frequently gay, lesbian, and bi trans people are only recognized for our oppressed sexuality. For example, at times when I've spoken to an audience largely made up of masculine, cross-dressing females, the media describes the audience as "predominantly lesbian" – rather than transgender – alluding only to their presumed sexual desire.

Many butch females and feminine males have been asked repeatedly why they seem to "attract" problems that other lesbians and gays do not. When we are unable to answer that question, personal shame burrows deeper into our battered bodies. The rise of trans liberation has given us the language to say, "I am oppressed because of my gender expression, as well as my sexuality."

Of the millions of masculine females and feminine males in this country, a percentage is bisexual, gay, and lesbian. How big a chunk? As long as same-sex love and bisexuality can get you fired, evicted, beaten up, or thrown into jail, we won't know. But much of the language of old gay life reflects gay gender outlaws: bulldaggers, nellies, butches, queens, diesel dykes, Marys, he-shes, she-males, drag kings, drag queens.

And we can say with certainty that gay trans people helped shape the modern lesbian, gay, and bi movement. Gay trans people were, and still are, some of the fiercest fighters on the front lines for lesbian, gay, and bi liberation.

However, I've heard the argument that lesbians, gays, and bisexuals have no connection to trans liberation because the majority of the trans population is heterosexual. Is that a valid reason to reject an alliance? I don't believe so.

We didn't build the gay liberation movement based on the specifics of what any of us do with consenting sexual partners. Instead, we fought to defend our sexual freedom, and to fight the discrimination and violence we face because of our sexuality. And those oppressions are inextricably linked with trans liberation. In a society in which heterosexuality *and* male / female dress and behavior are decreed and enforced by law, gay, lesbian, bisexual, and trans people are all gender transgressors.

There are no boundaries between the territories in which we live; our populations overlap. We cannot separate the demands for lesbian, gay, bisexual, and trans liberation.

We have our own pasts, and yet our histories have commingled. Wherever oppression has reared its ugly head, we have been thrown together into jail cells and concentration camps by cops, prosecutors, judges, and military brass who view us as guilty of the same crime: "queerness." Many anti-*gay* laws used over the centuries have targeted *feminine* gay males and *masculine* lesbians. And heterosexual cross-dressers have been jailed for being gay.

Today every lesbian woman, gay man, and bisexual person has to at some point deal with their relationship to sex and gender oppression. After all, the laws against same-sex marriage are based on the premise that sexual desire for the "opposite sex" is innate and natural. So loving someone of the same sex, or feeling sexual attraction to multiple sexes, is considered to be an illegal gender deviation. Yet lesbians, gays, and bisexuals are living proof that being born with a particular set of genitals does not automatically determine who you want to have caress them.

How many women who came out to friends or family have been told "At least you're not one of those cigar-smoking diesel dykes," or been asked, "Which one is the man?" How many gay and bisexual men have been told, "At least you're not some limp-wristed sissy in a dress," or "Don't let him treat you like the woman!"

That's gender-phobia and trans-phobia. It's sexist as hell, too! These are fears and prejudices that a person might deviate from the dress and behavior assigned to them at birth. But genitalia, sexual desire, gender expression, identification with one sex or another — one does not determine all the others. Human beings are not Rubic cubes.

So how do we answer those who hurl these backward questions at us? If you sigh in relief and answer "No, I'm not like *those* people," will you be in a stronger position or a weaker one? If you assure the world that you're not like us, then you've just locked yourself into having to super-conform to gender roles and stereotypes. Why do I say *super*-conform? Because you'll know you're under greater scrutiny because of your sexuality. That's a life sentence in a gender straightjacket.

And what about those millions of us who *are* cigar-smoking

butches and limp-wristed femmes? Those who prey on us and try to dismantle our civil rights will come for you next. Won't we all be stronger in a diverse movement in which each of our rights and our lives are defended by collective power?

We will all benefit from seeing the interconnectedness of our struggles and our histories. What unites us is not that we all express our sexuality in identical ways. If you doubt that, thumb through some of the personal ads in our community presses! It's not necessary to find a commonality in our sexuality. Unlike dairy products, sexuality absolutely does not need to be homogenized.

Defense of bisexual inclusion, for example, has strengthened our movement. We have formed a struggle alliance with another group of people fighting to defend their lives and their love.

Yet bisexuality embraces a vast swath of humanity, with diverse expressions of sexuality. This inclusion has opened up a greater understanding that bisexual people can't be forced into such formalistic categories as "half gay and half straight." People continue to be bisexual, or omnisexual, no matter who their partners are at any given time. The Draconian legal and social enforcement of heterosexuality makes no allowance for being "half-straight."

Bi inclusion in the coalition with lesbians and gay is not a question of uniting around "a common sexuality." And neither is trans inclusion. The trans populations span the spectrum of sexualities. And the lesbian, gay, and bi populations reflect all the variations of gender and sex.

Whenever a new fight against oppression emerges, some people have conflicting feelings. They know that a struggle against any form of bigotry and discrimination is ultimately good for everyone.

But they feel anxious about how those changes will affect their own lives and identities.

The sexuality of some trans people cannot be easily categorized. When the borders of sex and gender are not fixed, neither is the definition of what constitutes gay or lesbian or bisexual. That's exactly what scares some people about trans liberation. They feel like the earth is shifting under their feet: "Here we've finally established communities and a movement for women who love women and men who love men, and trans people seem to turn all that upside down."

That's why some people fear trans inclusion. They are afraid they'll no longer have any turf to stand on. And so they fear losing those lesbian/gay borders. But it's important to remember that those demarcations do not depend on being able to clearly define each *individual* as lesbian or gay. These rough boundaries delineate the scope of oppression; these are the perimeters of *collective* fight-back.

Trans liberation is not a threat to any lesbian woman or gay man or bisexual person. Yes, trans liberation is shaking up old patterns of thoughts or beliefs. Good! Because most of those thoughts and beliefs that we are challenging were imposed on us from above, were rotten to the core and were backed up by bigoted laws. But we're not taking away your identity. No one's sex reassignment or fluidity of gender threatens your right to self-identity and self-expression. On the contrary, our struggle bolsters your right to your identity. My right to be me is tied with a thousand threads to your right to be you.

We're not trying to barricade the road you travel; we're trying to open up more avenues to self-definition, and identity and love and sexuality. That's a wonderful development for everybody.

What unites us is not a common sexuality or experiences or identities or self-expression. It's that we are up against a common enemy. And this inter-relatedness of our struggles is not simply an outgrowth of contemporary Western society. The fight-back of sexually- and gender-oppressed peoples in class-divided societies has historically overlapped.

In London, 300 years before the Stonewall Rebellion, police routinely raided "molly houses"—clubs frequented by feminine, cross-dressed males who were presumed to be gay. During one raid in London in 1725, the crowd—many of them in drag—fought pitched battles with the police.

And like the Stonewall Rebellion, the German Homosexual Emancipation Movement — which began near the end of the last century — was an important example of one of the historic moments when lesbian, gay, and trans demands and leadership have entwined.

What is the most effective strategy to forge a fight-back movement today? Should we deny our relationship to each other based on relative difference and try to place an arm's distance between us? It sounds absurd. And yet there are some lesbians and gay men, I know, who fear that their "winnable" demands for legislative reforms or acceptance will be lost if they stand up for the rights of trans people.

"Let us win our demands first," they plead, "and then your demands will be more easily won later on." That's a trickle-down theory of reform. But those of us who have been trickled on in the past are not impressed with that strategy.

When a young social movement breaks down societal closet

doors and floods into the streets, its leading activists suddenly begin to get advice from those in power who were never "friendly" before. These advisors urge leaders to send in their "best-dressed, most articulate spokespeople" (code words for white and middle- to upper-classed) to negotiate for progressive legislation and other reforms. But, they counsel, "Keep it to a single, simple demand. And disassociate with those who are too angry and too militant."

This is an old tactic. When I was a teenager involved in factory struggles in Buffalo, New York, management sent similar messages through emissaries to union activists. But it was divisive – because the relationship of strength at the bargaining table is directly related to the relationship of forces on the picket lines outside. When we fought a list of demands together, kept each other's spirits high on the picket lines, and defended each other from attacks by cops and company goons, we frequently won.

But when we allowed ourselves to be split along lines of oppression, we always lost.

"An injury to one is an injury to all." It's the truth the union movement was built on. It's solid bedrock to build a lesbian, gay, bisexual, and trans liberation movement on, too. And it reminds us of our connection to others who are fighting for justice and equality.

We are not just gay, lesbian, bi or trans people. Our populations include many oppressed nationalities, people with AIDS, women, youths, elders, people who are unemployed, homeless, Deaf, disabled, prisoners, people dependent on welfare, SSI, Medicaid, and Medicare.

Today we are witnessing a violent bipartisan attack on all our standards of living. This slash-and-burn policy will affect millions of people all over the country, including many lesbian, gay, bi, and trans people. Is it any wonder that we are seeing a simultaneous rise in scapegoating?

Listen to the sound of bombs detonating at a lesbian bar in Atlanta – a bar that welcomed bisexual, gay, and trans people and other allies. Hear politicians – from the Oval office to the halls of Congress – vilifying and denouncing our love. Feel the repercussion of bomb blasts and bullets fired at women's health clinics. Smell the smoke from African-American churches, burned at a rate not seen since the violent counter-revolution against Black Reconstruction over a century ago. See the outlines of swastikas defacing Jewish homes and synagogues.

This divisive ideological blitz is mandatory in order to ram through these dramatic cuts in our standards of living and our social services. None of us can fight back alone and hope to win, no matter how much we sacrifice or how hard we struggle.

Who can we turn to? Who are our allies?

The lesbian, gay, bi, and trans communities are natural allies. Throughout the last decade in the United States, we have been stronger wherever we have formed coalitions – on campuses, in work places, and in political protests.

And everyone who is under the gun of reaction and economic violence is a potential ally. What an opportunity lesbian, gay, bi, and trans people have to play a leading role in the mass movements that must be organized to meet these attacks head-on. Our communities bring with us the lessons of militant struggle.

We can develop multi-issue coalitions with everyone who's struggling for social equality and economic justice. When people from different walks of life find themselves together in a collective protest, later they remember who stood tall with them when times were tough. That's how genuine solidarity is forged.

An injury to one is an injury to all! When we allow ourselves to be split along lines of oppression, we always lose. But when we put forward a collective list of demands together, and fight to defend each other from attacks, we frequently win.

SYLVIA RIVERA

*"I'm glad I was in the
Stonewall riot"*

*Sylvia Rivera was a combatant at the Stone-
wall Rebellion in June 1969 that sparked the young gay liberation movement. Sylvia Rivera and African-American drag queen Marsha Johnson co-
founded STAR: Street Transvestite Action Revolutionaries in New York
City in 1970. I asked Sylvia to describe her memories of life on the streets
of New York as a drag queen, the uprising in Greenwich Village, and the
era that followed:*

I left home at age ten in 1961. I hustled on 42nd Street. The early 60s
was not a good time for drag queens, effeminate boys or boys that wore
makeup like we did. Back then we were beat up by the police, by everybody. I didn't really come out as a drag queen until the late 60s.

When drag queens were arrested, what degradation there was. I
remember the first time I got arrested, I wasn't even in full drag. I was
walking down the street and the cops just snatched me. We always felt
that the police were the real enemy. We expected nothing better than to
be treated like we were animals – and we were. We were stuck in a bullpen
like a bunch of freaks. We were disrespected. A lot of us were beaten up
and raped. When I ended up going to jail, to do 90 days, they tried to rape
me. I very nicely bit the shit out of a man. I was an evil queen. I was strung
out on dope.

I've been through it all.

In 1969, the night of the Stonewall riot it was a very hot, muggy night.
We were in the Stonewall and the lights came on. We all stopped danc-
ing. The police came in. They had gotten their payoff earlier in the week.
But Inspector Pine came in – him and his Morals Squad – to spend more
of the government's money.

We were led out of the bar and they cattled us all up against the police vans. The cops pushed us up against the grates and the fences. People started throwing pennies, nickels, and quarters at the cops, and then the bottles started. And then we finally had the Morals Squad barricaded in the Stonewall building because they were actually afraid of us at that time. They didn't know we were going to react that way.

We were not taking any more of this shit. We had done so much for other movements. It was time. It was street gay people from the Village out front – homeless people who lived in the park in Sheridan Square outside the bar – and then drag queens behind them and everybody behind us. The Stonewall Inn telephone lines were cut and they were left in the dark.

One *Village Voice* reporter was in the bar at that time and according to the archives of the *Village Voice*, he was handed a gun from Inspector Pine and told "We got to fight our way out of here." This was after one Molotov cocktail was thrown and we were ramming the door of the Stonewall bar with an uprooted parking meter. So they were ready to come out shooting that night. Finally the Tactical Police Force showed up after 45 minutes. A lot of people forget that for 45 minutes we had them trapped in there.

All of us were working for so many movements at that time. Everyone was involved with the women's movement, the peace movement, the Civil Rights movement. We were all radicals. I believe that's what brought it around. You get tired of being just pushed around. We are people. We are gay people.

STAR came about after a sit-in at Weinstein Hall at New York University in 1970. Later we had a chapter in New York, one in Chicago, one in California and England. STAR was for the street gay people, the street homeless people, and anybody that needed help at that time. Marsha and I had always sneaked people into our hotel rooms. Marsha and I decided to get a building. We were trying to get away from the Mafia's control at the bars. And you can sneak 50 people into two hotel rooms. We got a building at 213 East 2nd Avenue. Marsha and I just decided it was time to help each other and help our other kids. We fed people and clothed people. We kept the building going. We went out and hustled the streets. We paid the rent. We didn't want the kids out in the streets hustling. They would go out and rip off food. There was always food in the house and everyone had fun. It lasted for 2 or 3 years.

We would sit there and ask, "Why do we suffer?" As we got more involved into the movements, we said, "Why do we always got to take the brunt of this shit?"

Later on, when the Young Lords came about in New York City, I was already in GLF (Gay Liberation Front). There was a mass demonstration that started in East Harlem in the fall of 1970. The protest was against police repression and we decided to join the demonstration with our STAR banner. That was one of the first times the STAR banner was shown in public, where STAR was present as a group. I ended up meeting some of the Young Lords that day. I became one of them. Any time they needed any help, I was always there for the Young Lords. It was just the respect they gave us as human beings. They gave us a lot of respect. It was a fabulous feeling for me to be myself – being part of the Young Lords as a drag queen – and my organization [STAR] being part of the Young Lords.

I met [Black Panther Party leader] Huey Newton at the Peoples' Revolutionary Convention in Philadelphia in 1971. Huey decided we were part of the revolution – that we were revolutionary people.

I was a radical, a revolutionist. I am still a revolutionist. I was proud to make the road and help change laws and what not. I was very proud of doing that and proud of what I'm still doing, no matter what it takes.

Today, we have to fight back against the government. We have to fight them back. They're cutting back Medicaid, cutting back on medicine for people with AIDS. They want to take away from women on welfare and put them into that little work program. They're going to cut SSI. Now they're taking away food stamps. These people who want the cuts – these people are making millions and millions and millions of dollars as CEOS. Why is the government going to take it away from us? What they're doing is cutting us back. Why can't we have a break!

I'm glad I was in the Stonewall riot. I remember when someone threw a Molotov cocktail, I thought, "My god, the revolution is here. The revolution is finally here!" I always believed that we would have a fight back. I just knew that we would fight back. I just didn't know it would be that night. I am proud of myself as being there that night. If I had lost that moment, I would have been kinda hurt because that's when I saw the world change for me and my people.

Of course, we still got a long way ahead of us.

"I'm taking it to a different level, beyond categorization"

So many of us are confused by gender – our own and others. One of the characters in my current novel-in-progress, *SisterGirl,* Iaisha Jeremiah Lamentations Ezekiel Gates, who currently lives in Europe, puts it this way:

"It seemed like all a Black Queen could do in the States was a coupla shows in some seedy bars or sell her ass on the street. Oh, no, trust, honey, trust, the guardian angels spared me from ever having to sale my ass on the streets to get by. But I hung around that scene for some years. I suppose things must be changing back there a little bit. I saw RuPaul in Miami Beach last summer, and Miss Supermodel of the World has taken Black Queendom to a new level. I was like you better woooooork, bitch! Didn't surprise me at all, Miss Girl, that if a drag queen were to take over the world, it would be a Black one.

"I started doing drag because I felt it was easier to fall off that edge onto the woman side, seeing as I was so damned sissified anyway. But I don't need to tell you that. One thing I noticed about the mustachioed B-boys and nappy-headed hoodlums – who looked like they were trying to be men harder than I was trying to be woman – was that they never gave me no shit. I could walk in the roughest neighborhoods of any city, and though I was serving up true banji cunt realness (I mean passing as a woman – that's just some language left over from Harlem ball lingo – folk tell me I need to get that out of my vocab, it's got those misogynist overtones, but you know, it takes a while to change speech patterns, much less whole phrases), there was no way folks could look at these big-ass feet of mine, alternating between my best feature and biggest giveaway, and think I was born with anything else between my legs but a monkey. But then again, folk can be as blind as they need to be in order to get along in this here life without getting their faces cracked. Aside from a remark now and then by some old drunken fool, I realized folk dealt with me straight up because they one: thought they could buy a piece (and that was usually the roughest of the rough necks); two: they saw some- one not to be fucked with; or three: they regarded me as a joke, a clown, a caricature to be dismissed as quick as a bad trick. It wasn't that I didn't truly feel like a man, or wanted to have my mojo permanently removed or something like that. Most times, in fact, I felt more aggressive and con- frontational in my pumps than my combat boots.

"Back then, I don't think I knew, in my head anyway, what the allure of femininity was all about or where it could lead me. These days, I can look at the young Black men in any American city, and they either hiding from themselves in some oversized, baggy B-boy drag, caps turned backward or hoods pulled so low over their faces they look like Klan, wasting time on corners looking like they're up to no good – and usually ain't – or I see the young Black boys who want to be in the life, but before they can even say 'Gay,' they got those lips lined in black, their nails done in Night-glo red, and they've spent a fortune on some new hair.

"Mine is a strand to strand honey, the most expensive kind. In my work, I can't afford nothing cheap. But you know what I'm trying to say. It's like the young Queens ran, just like me, from their maleness to find a comfort, a safety, if you will, in their femaleness. Not like anything neg- ative should be said about the other away around, but I know you know for us Black folk, it seems like what we have constructed to be repre- sentative of Black men is going to be much harder for the folk on the edges of gender to play than it is to play what we have come to exalt as the strong, independent, Black woman. When you get right down to it, gender is performance, darling. Anybody that can't see that got they weave in too tight. As a performer professionale, I'm taking it to a different level, beyond categorization, but folk are running around performing gender off-stage as well. This notion hit me like cold water, when, for a hot minute, I thought about goin all the way, you know, getting rid of the monkey. I must admit, I did consider hormones and surgery. But I finally realized, even though you need a pussy to be female, you sure as hell don't need one to be woman. Besides, I wasn't no fool in school, and from what I can remember from Biology or Physiology, or whichever it was, we were all conceived as females anyway. I swear it – honey, I'd bet this weave on it – there's a little Black girl or a big Black woman inside of everyone. Either you let her breath, or you try to smother her. So, Miss Jones, as you used to say, 'Put that up in your pipe and smoke it!' "

7.

Learning from Experience

The City University of New York (CUNY) auditorium was packed with young people. I was about to deliver the address that would close the 7th Annual Queer Graduate Studies Conference. The theme of the conference was "Forms of Desire." The organizers told me they'd asked me to speak about the basis for unity between the struggles of lesbian, gay, bi, and trans communities on- and off-campus.

I looked out over the young students, most of whom relied on financial aid and part-time jobs to stay in school. I knew many wondered if they would end up working at the Gap or flipping hamburgers after leaving graduate school. Their sexual desires were still illegal in many states; they could be bashed on the streets for holding hands.

It wasn't hard to see where our lives and our struggles connected.

I am particularly pleased because I am addressing two audiences today: members of the Queer graduate communities and those from the lesbian, gay, bi, and trans communities off-campus. I have tremendous confidence in the power that we can unleash by uniting our struggles.

When I talk about unity, I don't mean reducing all our particular identities or struggles to one. I mean putting our collective strength and energy behind the defense of *all* our identities and *all* our demands.

That's why I want to compliment the organizers who named this conference "Forms of Desire," for making *form* plural! Even a conference made up solely of self-identified lesbians or gay men or bisexuals would require a plural title. Our sexualities are diverse and complex.

And the plural *forms* also allows us as transgender and transsexual and intersexual people to represent and express our own desires. For some time, trans theory and history have been thought of as part and parcel of lesbian and gay theory and history. But we must define our own paths and experiences. In doing so, we lay the basis for greater understanding of where our populations, issues, and struggles connect.

The use of the title "Forms of Desire" for this conference also inspires us to reconceptualize the relationship of lesbian, gay, bi, and trans desires to other desires that are discriminated against, debased, and deferred.

How do we fight on behalf of all our desires? I believe that exploring the relationship between theory, history, and action will help answer that question.

I can't even begin to talk about the relationship of history and theory without trying to demystify both categories. History is the record of past experience. Theory is the generalization of that experience. It's that simple. But the question of who records the experience, and what lessons are drawn from it, is not so simple. Theory and history take place in the midst of a struggle, and are themselves battlegrounds.

Take theory, for example. Most working people think theory,

in general, doesn't have much to do with real life. With some theories, that's true. Theory that strays too far from experience becomes abstract – an idealist argument about how many angels can dance on the head of a pin. Theory has to be tested against reality.

While carefully studying questions of sex and gender oppression, or the oppression of same-sex or omni-sexual love, we have to be careful not to produce theoretical hothouse flowers that are removed from the social and economic soil in which they are rooted.

And since theory is the generalization of experience, we have to ask: Whose experience is it? From whose point of view?

The dominant theories in any society reflect the economic interests of those who dominate the society. How can it be otherwise? Who pays an army of spin-doctors and public relations experts to try to mold popular opinion? Who determines educational curricula? Who owns and controls the monopolized television, publishing, and media? The cacophony of theorists hired to defend the status quo is meant to drown out the voices of those who are fighting for change.

That's why we must ask everyone who puts forward theory: Which side are you on?

Theory is important to those of us who are struggling to transform society because it offers distilled experience so we don't have to repeat mistakes. A scientific materialist view of theory and history gives working and oppressed peoples a roadmap to find the path toward liberation.

For revolutionaries, theory that is not a guide to action is a worthless intellectual exercise. Our analysis has to be as taut as a diving board that enables us to springboard into the fray, to be able to recognize allies and enemies, and put an end to economic inequality and social injustice altogether.

Struggle informs theory, and theory in turn counsels action. That's why those at the summits of power do everything they can to ridicule and condemn and censor these ideas.

I am part of a revolutionary current around the world that is trying to challenge and break with the old ruling theories.

For example, from the time I was a child, I was drilled in the theory that I lived in an upwardly-mobile classless society, in which anyone who is hardworking and enterprising can get rich.

But when I grew up, and began to use the theories of Marxism to look more closely at the society in which I lived, I saw that society is split asunder by class divisions. I, and everyone I knew, broke our backs every day working in the factories and fields. Did we get rich? Hell, no. We got another day older and deeper in debt.

But the tiny owning class that claims all the factories and fields are their private property did get richer – off our labor. Each day that we worked so long and so hard to produce goods and services, we were not paid the full value of our day's labor. The chunk of value we were not paid became the owners' profits. Multiply those profits times 365 days a year, and times more than 100 million workers in the United States – and that's how the rich get richer.

Editorial writers at the *Wall Street Journal* or *Financial Times* can argue that this theory I've put forward is wrong. But then they have to disprove it. And they have to put forward another theory to explain why the rich get richer and the poor get poorer – and prove that their theory can stand up to the test of reality.

Keep your eye on experience because that's what theory is all about. It's like the Hale-Bopp comet. If one group of scientists argues that the comet will appear at this point in time, and another group says it won't, check the night sky just after sunset or before dawn and see whose theory lights up the sky.

Recognizing the struggle between these two major classes in society – those who work for a living, and those who get rich off our labor – shapes my approach to theoretical questions.

For example, I've heard the academic argument that transgender is a revolutionary tactic in the struggle against the patriarchy, but that transsexual men and women uphold the oppressive either-or categories of man and woman.

That's not true. And it's an example of a theory that pits transgender and transsexual people against each other.

First of all, we don't don transgender like a Batman costume to go out and do battle with the patriarchy. This is not a tactic; these are our lives we are fighting for.

And the shorthand use of *patriarchy* is sloppy. The rule of which men? John D. Rockefeller or Nat Turner? If the use of patriarchy means, more accurately, the wealthy male-dominated owning class, then it's still not clear why transgenderism is revolutionary and transsexualism is not.

Every patriarchal ruling class – from the slave-owning Caesars to the feudal landlords to the modern barons of banking and industry – have partitioned the sexes by designating all infants either male or female at birth and also by mandated "sex-appropriate" clothing and behavior. So how is the bridging or blurring of that divide by transgenderists any more of a challenge to this repressive system than the challenge to birth sex assignment by transsexuals?

And why does this attack on the right of transsexuals to live as women or men always seem to come from non-transsexual individuals who themselves identify as women or men? Holding trans-sexual men and women responsible for the man-woman binary is tantamount to accusing anyone who uses a public toilet with a gendered stick figure on the door of upholding patriarchal paternity and inheritance.

It's true that this binary system is repressive. But what is so restrictive about it is that it brutally tries to force all human variance into two tiny categories. It's not true that the only revolutionary position is to fight from outside that system. People who identify as women and men can wage an important defense of the right to other identities. And vice versa!

The argument that it's reactionary to identify as a woman or a man is not a new one. In the 1970s, I remember hearing that androgyny was the only revolutionary position from which to fight the repressive social values attached to being masculine or feminine. That was not true either. We all have the right to find our place on the circle of sex and gender, and still defend every other point on its circumference.

As with theory, many working-class children—especially the poorest and most oppressed—are taught early on to tune out discussions of history. We're told that's for "smart" people, for intellectuals.

This insulting attitude results in righteous working-class anger directed at intellectuals as people who think they are "better" than we are. But blue-collar rejection of intellectualism is a double-edged sword, because it can obscure the need for the development of working-class intellectuals.

Imagine the hypocrisy of telling us that we cannot possibly understand history! It's always been the toiling classes who have swept onto the historical arena and ushered in great change. We are making history now in our workplaces, on our campuses, in our communities.

That is why a conference like this one, that reexamines what we are fighting for, and what we're up against, and who our allies are, is important to help keep us on track. And that's why history — as a record of past experiences — is so important.

For example, history offers an overview of past economic systems. Don't those of us who are suffering most in this unequal economic system need that information in order to discuss how we could fight for a new form of social organization?

History, in the hands of those who have the most to gain from change, is a formidable weapon. That's why the colonizers and imperialists always burned and destroyed the historical accounts of those they conquered. They revise history to parrot one message over and over again: "The way things are now is the way they've always been." The meaning is clear and demoralizing: Don't even think about fighting for change.

History is recorded from the point of view of the hunter or the hunted. And that is why, in the words of a wise African proverb: Until the lions come to power, the hunters write the history.

The stereotype of historians as sitting on a pastoral fence, observing and reporting events objectively, doesn't exist in reality. History is a chronicle of struggles. The fences are barricades. And barricades are a dangerous and impossible place to perch on during a battle.

So the question we must demand of historians is: Which side are you on?

For those of us engaged in a struggle to change society, unearthing buried history can make a real activist contribution. I saw this during the 1960s and 1970s, when African Americans, Latinos, Native nations, women, lesbians, gays, and others were striving to overturn the most repressive laws and institutions. When oppressed people dug up a more accurate historical account, their roles in history – previously rendered invisible – were revealed. This helped shed light on the relationship between economic exploitation and oppression. And those who saw they were fighting a common enemy recognized each other as allies.

This previously suppressed history offered a renewed strength and clarity that enabled movements against oppression to exert more powerful demands on cultural and educational institutions. African American, Chicano and Native American Studies, Women's Studies, Lesbian and Gay, Gender and Queer Studies are victories wrested through those militant struggles.

That's just one example of the impact of history on struggle and of struggle on history.

As trans people, we also need the lessons of the past in order to help us grapple with present political issues. For example, how can we respond to the recent media gender-phobic frenzy about whether New York City Mayor Rudolph Giuliani is a cross-dresser? This is not the first time, or the last, that this particular problem of a hated political figure being labeled or outed as trans will have to be answered by progressive people.

As many of you know, the Mayor appeared in a dress in a skit at the annual Inner Circle event in Manhattan. Oh, the political pundits and prognosticators were all atwitter. Why, they asked, did hizzoner appear as Rudia in a pink spangled ballgown and gold spike heels? If the skit was a prank, why wasn't it crude and slapstick?

Giuliani's makeup was meticulously applied, his blond bouffant wig carefully coifed.

The media quoted horrified politicians: "How can I look Giuliani in the face again? What was he thinking? Doesn't he care about his political future?"

These questions skirted two important issues.

First, Giuliani is a reactionary politician who deserves to be hated for busting unions, slashing social services, and unleashing a wave of police terror – not for cross-dressing. And second, why should anyone be disturbed because a man dons a dress?

The only historical context that I read in the media was a *New York Times* editorial about Giuliani's drag appearance. The editorial recalled that Lord Edward Cornbury, who governed New York and New Jersey on behalf of the British Crown in the early eighteenth century, wore gowns to everything from formal dances to his wife's funeral. Letters to the editor countered these "charges" were merely political mudslinging.

This debate did little to create a historical context for transgender.

My own research has led me to believe that trans expression is not rooted in a modern reaction to restricted sex and gender roles in class-divided societies. I have documented that trans expression predates such oppression. Gender variance, sex change, and intersexuality appear to have existed globally throughout the history of human societies.

There was a material basis for the respect and honor accorded to sex and gender diversity in ancient societies that relied on cooperative labor. And that makes sense, because the essential glue of teamwork is recognition of the value each individual brings to the group.

Once human society severed into haves and have-nots, trans expression continued to exist in both antagonistic classes. But only the small owning class that ruled over the vast majority had a powerful economic motive to create difference from diversity, and use it as a weapon to sow division. Those at the summits of wealth, and their representatives, will resort to gender-phobic and homophobic attacks, even if they themselves are transgender and/or gay.

Take, for example, the late but not lamented former FBI director J. Edgar Hoover. He was reportedly a gay cross-dresser. But he was a rabid pitbull hired to defend capitalism. In the 1970s Hoover waged a dirty war, known as COINTELPRO, against anyone who fought for revolutionary change, including left-wing lesbian and gay activists—many of whom were cross-dressers, Black Panthers, Young Lords, and others.

Before the Stonewall Rebellion, lesbian, gay, bisexual, and trans activists had been active, and provided leadership, in battles against oppression – building the union movement, organizing tenants, defending the Scottsboro Brothers, challenging the anti-communist McCarthy hearings, organizing for a stay of execution for the Rosenbergs, swelling the ranks of the Civil Rights movement. But the demand for lesbian and gay liberation had not yet been voiced, let alone bisexual and trans demands. So most were in the closet about their own sex or gender oppression.

However, the growth of these movements helped the Stonewall Rebellion and gay liberation to emerge. Each movement that challenged oppression made more room for another.

Many of the early trans and gay activists – because we were part of left-wing movements – were steeled in the training and skills, tactics and strategy necessary to carry out a massive struggle. And because we had ties to these other movements, we understood the need for solidarity.

Almost immediately after the Stonewall Rebellion, the flags and banners of lesbian and gay liberation proudly flew at demonstrations in defense of the Black Panther Party, Young Lords, the American Indian Movement, and the United Farm Workers. The Gay Liberation Front took its name in solidarity with the Vietnamese National Liberation Front.

By bringing the demands of our liberation movement to people from all walks of life, we deepened mass consciousness of the need for unity. And this also impacted on other movements.

In 1970, Black Panther leader Huey Newton issued a historic statement declaring, "When we have revolutionary conferences, rallies, and demonstrations there should be full participation of the gay liberation movement and the women's liberation movement." Newton urged revolutionaries not to use anti-gay slurs to express their hatred of "men who are enemies of the people, such as Nixon." Newton stressed, "Homosexuals are not enemies of the people."

Months after the Stonewall Rebellion, the Young Lords in New York City formed an internal Lesbian and Gay Caucus. One of its founding members was Puerto Rican drag queen Sylvia Rivera, who fought at Stonewall. Rivera, together with Stonewall-combatant Marsha Johnson, formed STAR — Street Transvestite Action Revolutionaries — to fight for the right of the most oppressed young drag queens to food, housing, health care, employment, and against racism and police brutality.

This is an important chapter in history. It's full of lessons for progressives and revolutionaries of all generations. But it's a chapter that's missing from textbooks around the country.

So perhaps the greatest contribution that any of us can make who excavate history, and who develop and clarify theory, is to ensure that our history and theory is relevant and accessible to all those who are ready and willing to take action.

I began by saying I felt confidence in the strength we can gain by connecting our issues and our struggles – on campus and off. The history of the battle for open admissions in the CUNY system supports my certainty.

Some of you may not know that, in 1969, Black and Latino students seized the south campus of City College in uptown Manhattan to demand an open admissions policy. CUNY was tuition free at that time. So why was the demand for open admissions pressed so militantly? The community college was technically free, but admissions were restricted. Although the campus was smack in the middle of Harlem, the student body was more than 85 percent white. The mechanism of control was grade point minimums and SAT scores.

Locking students from working poor and oppressed families out of college began with the tracking of students from the first days of junior high and high schools. Students weighed down by segregated schools, inferior education, lack of resources, and the need to hold down a job, had a hard time lifting up their grade point average.

CUNY was free to all. Technically. But in reality admissions were restricted. Not by law, but by fact.

And so, in the spring of 1969, Black and Latino students wrote their own impressive chapter in history. The City College south campus was enclosed with iron gates to keep out the Harlem community. But the students occupied the campus, and renamed the occupied territory "Harlem U." They opened up the gates for classes and workshops for the community.

The college and the New York City administration were afraid to order a police assault. The students were militant, and the Harlem community supported the occupation. The authorities remembered the wave of rebellions across the country just a year before, after Dr. Martin Luther King, Jr., was assassinated.

The students held the campus for weeks. By summer, they won their demand that any student with a high school diploma be guaranteed a place in the CUNY system. And they won an expansion of the SEEK program and academic remedial help to alleviate the consequences of discriminatory education.

This struggle was an outgrowth of the Civil Rights and Black liberation movements. It was fueled by protests and rebellions across the country against racism and the Pentagon war against Vietnam. The women's liberation movement was on the rise. In turn, the battle for CUNY open admissions waged by the Black and Latino students spread to other colleges, and won multinational support.

And at the same time students were winning their fight on the south campus in Harlem, the Stonewall Rebellion exploded a few miles downtown.

Today, how do the struggles of students, faculty, and campus employees overlap with those of us battling off-campus? We are all the targets of a bipartisan war on our wages, our social services, and our civil rights. Only those who have not been the victims of the first volleys could think this is an exaggeration.

Access to education is under attack. Private colleges and universities – like other profit-driven corporations – are laying off workers, busting unions, cutting costs, and boasting record profits. Classrooms are overcrowded. Tuition costs are soaring while financial aid is plummeting. Tenured professors are axed, and replaced with adjuncts. Graduate employees work long hours without benefits just to cover their tuition.

Super-exploitative chains like McDonald's and Barnes & Noble are used as outsourcers to replace organized food service, bookstore, and other campus employees.

We're experiencing a similarly reactionary offensive off-campus against every program and social service won through struggle. Slashing welfare has plunged millions more children and women into poverty. Documented immigrants who have paid taxes for years are suddenly finding their elderly parents are being thrown out of nursing homes, and parents of disabled children are losing the food stamps that helped keep their families from starving.

Medicare, Medicaid, and SSI, services for people with AIDS, youths and elders, drug treatment clinics – all of it is on the chopping block.

Why are these cuts necessary? Because the budget deficit is mushrooming out of control? No, the budget deficit is dramatically shrinking.

Is it because we are in the midst of an economic depression? No, this has been a period of so-called economic recovery.

Is it because the United States is sinking in competitive relation to other capitalist countries? No, the U.S. economy is thriving in relation to Japan and Europe. Our labor in this country has created an economy valued at $7 trillion per year.

These social services are being gutted because Corporate

America – more accurately Corporate North America – thinks that with the help of their paid politicians, and their begowned lawyers on the Supreme Court, they can get away with a massive theft of wealth from the poor and working-class and middle-income people.

They are already surfeited with record profits reaped from the restructuring of the capitalist economy. But for us this "leaner, meaner" economy has meant layoffs, speed-ups, and loss of benefits.

It's no accident that at the same moment this economic offensive is taking hold, we are witnessing an offensive against affirmative action and multicultural curricula, under the banner of war on "political correctness." The success of such a frontal attack on the broad majority of people could surely generate mass resistance. That's why it's necessary for those responsible for these antihuman measures to fan the flames of scapegoating and bigotry.

So when Clinton and other demagogues try to sell us their concept of a bridge to the twenty-first century, they really mean a bridge back to the nineteenth century!

This brings me to my final question: Is there a concrete basis for the unity required to forge a much larger movement, one capable of defending all of our rights, winning significant social and economic reforms, and even transforming society into an equitable system in which diversity is esteemed?

Absolutely. Unequivocally. Yes! Historical experience repeatedly demonstrates that it is just a matter of time before this movement explodes onto the stage of history.

But on what basis will we forge such a movement? Around what forms of desire? The ache of hunger? The desperate need of poverty and homelessness? The yearning for freedom from oppression? The longing for justice? The battle lines are already drawn. The stepped-up war on our most basic rights makes the barricades in this class war plainly visible.

On one side are the Goliaths of industry and banking, greedy to take back all the concessions won by mass struggles over the last six decades. On the other side is everyone who is being hurt by budget cuts, repression, bigotry, and poverty.

There are and will be lesbian, gay, bisexual, and trans people on both sides of these barricades. How do we recognize our allies from our enemies?

History and theory compel us to ask: Which side are you on?

WILLIAM MASON (PEACHES)

"I finally got that respect"

People are funny. All the years I was a Drag Queen people would look at me, roll their eyes, make nasty remarks. Boys would chase me and the girls hated me. Not all of them. I did have a few – very few – real true friends. Alls I wanted was to be loved and respected for the person that I was. But I guess respect has to be earned. I've been a respectful person all my life, but too many times, for too many reasons, it's not returned – up until about a year ago when a few of us formed an organization (Workfairness), an organization fighting for Rights for people on welfare or Public Assistance. At the time (and I still am on Public Assistance) I was on my WEP assignment when my supervisor said, "William, you can't sit here all day and do nothing, go in there and clean the men's room."

I felt totally disrespected being that I was assigned as an office clerk. Well the stuff hit the fan. Words started rolling out of my mouth so hard God covered his ears. (smile)

It's bad enough that you're on PA and most people think that people on PA are lazy and worthless, so they don't treat you with dignity or respect.

Well, I wasn't having it. My coworkers were afraid my case would be closed or something and said "William, we're so glad you told her off." Being oppressed and depressed people, sometimes we didn't respect each other.

Anyway enough of that. Now that I'm helping people on public assistance things have changed. Some of those same people that use to dis me now have found respect for me. People that need help don't care if you are a Drag Queen, Trans, Bi, Lesbian, or what. If you can help them, you get respect, teach them, you get respect, fight for them, you get respect.

I remember one day we went to a sanitation work site to get new members for Workfairness. As I was talking I could see and hear some of the guys laughing and saying, "Man, what does this homo think he can do? Who's going to take him seriously?"

I could sense that this could get ugly so I said to them, "If you are such big bad men where were you when I was shaking my fist and raising hell at City Hall fighting for your Rights? Pushing a broom somewhere. If I'm a Homo fighting for my right, show me how much man you are and join in this fight."

All of the men got quiet and the women too. The mood changed again. They all signed cards. Before I left they were shaking my hand and calling me Mr. Mason.

Things like that started happening at most sites we went on. People were coming to the Workfairness Center or calling asking for Mr. Mason, giving me the utmost Respect.

Well, I finally got that respect, thank you very much. But please, Drag Queens don't like being called Mr. Anything. So please respect me a little more and just call me William or Peaches. (smile)

WILLIAM/PEACHES IS A WORKFARE EXPERIENCE PROGRAM WORKER AND IS COCHAIR OF WORKFAIRNESS IN NEW YORK CITY.

8.

I am home, working at my computer. I can hear Minnie Bruce's keyboard clicking and clacking nearby as she puts the finishing touches on an epic poem.

As I reach the conclusion of this book, I am facing another springtime of travel. It is 1998. But the majority of my life is not spent at a podium, invited by people who respect my work. Instead, when I'm out in public, I spend far too much of my precious time and energy trying to find a safe public toilet, or negotiating my way past groups of hostile people who block my path. I spend a lot of time at the gym trying to work off the tension of being stared at — glared at — wherever I go. But I am considered an unwelcome intruder in either the women's or the men's dressing room in the health club.

Most days I feel very isolated — marginalized most places I go. Really, the only places in the world where I fit are the spaces that have been liberated by political struggles. That's what makes it possible for me to speak to students and faculty at universities and colleges, youth groups, community organizations, rallies, and demonstrations. A big chunk of my life is spent editing a weekly socialist newspaper, attending meetings, organizing Deaf and disabled accessibility for rallies, doing group childcare so that parent activists can attend protests, seal-

ing envelopes, faxing press releases, and leafleting at subway stops.

I spend much of my life doing volunteer grassroots organizing because I believe this is the way to win fundamental and lasting change for everyone, including myself, whose life is constricted or injured or disrespected by the system we live under.

Change. Most of us yearn for it. What kind of change do you want? What kind of change is trans liberation fighting for?

What are the goals of the trans movement?

It depends on who you ask. When a movement first begins to surge, many people from all walks of life who share that oppression rise up together and want to put forward one strong demand. But as the movement develops, many divergent ideas are voiced.

How could it be otherwise? I've sat in sleazy diners in the middle of the night listening to homeless teenage drag queens rage against the cops who beat them mercilessly and then demand sex, and against the system that won't cut them a single break. I've sat in conferences with cross-dressers who own banks and railroads, hold high-level government offices, and run television studios. What demands can all these trans people agree on? What definition of liberation? At what points will their political paths diverge?

Some of our issues are so sharply defined and clear we'd be hard pressed to debate them. For example, no matter how you identify yourself, I'm sure you and I agree the devaluation of trans lives must end. No one should be chased down the street or beaten bloody because of what they're wearing or how they define or present themselves. No one should be out of work, paid lower wages, or arbitrarily fired because of their identity. No one who is ill or injured should be turned away from medical care.

Should we stop there? I know I can't.

I feel the necessity to fight for the rights of transsexual men and women to respectful and affordable medical care, and to defend the right of intersexual people to make their own informed decisions about their own bodies. I stand up for every individual's right to their expression of gender, free from criticism or condemnation.

Trans people – everyone in fact – have a right to safe, sanitary, single-occupancy toilets. All trans people deserve identification papers that reflect our lives respectfully. Trans youths have a right to a home and an education; trans elders deserve sensitive care; trans prisoners need defense against prison officials who allow and encourage others to gang rape them.

If you do not identify as a trans person, you can make a significant contribution to our movement. I know many people who do not experience the oppression directly feel diminished and degraded by how trans people are treated. Thousands of people have told me, in conversations, e-mail, letters, and telephone calls, about the pain they felt in the pit of their stomach when a drag queen or transsexual or butch female was verbally harassed in public.

"I didn't know what to do," is what I hear most often. "I didn't want to embarrass the person or call more attention to them. What should I do the next time?" This is frequently the response of a caring, good-hearted person who was caught in a situation that they were never socially prepared for. Each of these people left the situation feeling shaken, emotionally raw, and powerless.

The answer is: There is no formula. There is only this guideline: What would you want a sympathetic stranger to do if you were in a similar situation? It's not easy to deflect the lightning bolts of hate and ridicule directed at one person toward yourself. It's not easy for anyone to stand up to a bully or bullies. You may stand completely alone with that trans person. Or that trans person, caught in the snare of public humiliation, may not even acknowledge your support.

But you may surprise yourself, too. You may tap into that seam of rocky courage that made you the honest, sensitive person you are today. You may inspire other strangers, temporarily silenced by fear, to speak up.

There are other fronts to this fight. Someone on the job might spark a confrontation, for example, because a transsexual coworker, who is transitioning from male-to-female, is using the women's bathroom. If you were in that situation, what you would want a coworker to do for you? You can offer to escort her to the bathroom, so everyone sees you are not buying into the fear being whipped up. You can dispel anxiety that transsexual women pose any danger to another woman. You can face down the loudest bigots, knowing that if trans-phobia goes unchallenged, sexism and anti-lesbian, gay, and bi prejudices will intensify, too.

Each friend and coworker and neighbor and family member you tell about your actions will be more prepared for the moment they defend a trans person. And you may discover that some of them had — or have — trans friends and lovers, but didn't know that you were an open enough person to be confided in. Our loved ones need every iota of support and solidarity that we as trans people do.

You may still leave these confrontations feeling rattled and raw. I know I do. But one thing is sure: You won't feel powerless. You will grow as a person who has come to grips with the fact that the way you are a woman or a man is one way to be, not the only way to be. You will have learned to spot bigotry in another cloaked form. Your pride and confidence in yourself will grow. And you will be a treasured ally.

So, what are the goals of trans liberation? There is not one single answer. If you ask me, the aim should not fall a yard short of genuine social and economic liberation for everyone. How to build a movement capable of achieving that objective, however, is the crux of the matter at hand.

Confronting all forms of gender-phobia and trans-phobia are very important to me. But I have worked hard all my life and have almost nothing to show for it. In large part because I am a visibly-identified trans person, I've had low-paying jobs that offer no pension and pay a pittance into Social Security. How will I survive as a blue-collar trans elder? I have to literally scrape together hundreds of dollars every month on health insurance. The urgent need for *affordable* health care is just as real for me as the need to tear down the brick walls of bigotry that block my access. Rent devours a bigger chunk of my income every year.

And I face many other struggles. For example, my partner and I have very few rights as a same-sex couple. I am female in a woman-hating society. And I am regularly confronted with anti-Semitism. The oppressions I battle are layered, and all weigh heavily on me.

We're still in the beginning stages of the trans movement. And so the question of what will be the consciousness of this movement is still up for grabs. How this question is settled will have long-term ramifications. Are we simply attempting to win legislative victories? As important as these reforms are, they do not address the root causes of trans oppression.

The majority of trans people suffer from police harassment,

assault, racism, sexism, high unemployment, low wages, job insecurity, homelessness, lack of health care, and high rents. The problem for trans people isn't just backward attitudes, it's the system. It's an economic system that is profit-driven – valuing only the bottom line – so people's needs always come last. This Robin-Hood-in-reverse system robs the poor to enrich a tiny fraction of the population. Yet that small wealthy class has learned in a highly refined way that the success to maintaining its rule is to split up the majority, make us point our fingers at one another, focus our anger at each other.

Our trans movement is getting stronger because we're fighting. But the progress that we've made is fragile. History teaches us that when an economic crisis hits, the process of scapegoating becomes more intense and more violent. African-American, Latino, Asian, and Arab peoples, lesbians, gay men, and bisexuals, feminists, trans people – and others who have been in the forefront of progress – will increasingly find themselves in the crosshairs. And the gains we made will all be under siege, as well.

To safeguard what we've won and to move forward requires securing, solidifying, and making more permanent alliances with others who are hurt by the same system. Consciousness plays an important role in cementing this coalition. Shared consciousness becomes a material force because what you're fighting for and what you are determined to win together has a big impact on how your foes react to you.

For example, if in the course of the Vietnam war the U.S. antiwar movement had only demanded negotiations, that would have been defined as the outer limit of the debate in this country.

But the consciousness of all the Vietnamese who were fighting the seemingly overwhelming Pentagon forces was that they weren't going to give up. They were going to fight to the death for their freedom. This determination of the Vietnamese had a profound impact on the consciousness of people in the United States. The growing consciousness here became: We don't want one more person to die!

The resolve of the Vietnamese and its effect on anti-war consciousness in the United States had a deep and pervasive impact on those who had the most to gain and the least to lose by refusing to fight – U.S. soldiers. By 1971, one out of four of all U.S. military soldiers worldwide – not just those in Vietnam – had either gone AWOL or deserted. And many other soldiers – individually and as groups – actively resisted the war in Vietnam, refused to put down rebellions in inner cities in the United States, held sit-down actions, fragged abusive officers, and participated in other acts of rebellion. The might of their combined consciousness made it very hard for the brass to conduct a war.

Or look at the consciousness of impoverished working-class people in the United States during the 1930s. People were so poor during the Depression that they were literally starving to death in the streets. They joined the ranks of massive protests and made it clear they were going to keep fighting until they got some justice. And that social upheaval resulted in the reform package known as the New Deal.

The Social Security Act wasn't passed because people lobbied politicians. It was passed because in cities across the country tens of thousands of unemployed people marched and rallied and waged militant strikes. When the landlords evicted tenants, organizing committees moved them back in; when the electric companies shut off people's lights and gas, progressive organizers came in and turned them back on. There was a growing radicalization – a rising tide of struggle.

And when people started to fight together in the mid-1930s on issues of economic and social security and the right to unionize, it brought Black/white unity to the fore. People needed each other in order to win their demands. As a result, the number of lynchings in this country plunged precipitously.

The Klan and lynchings were developed as barbarous weapons of counter-revolutionary terror to dismantle the tremendous social victories of African Americans during Black Reconstruction, and later to maintain an apartheid-like police state in the southern half of this country. Between 1866 and 1933 there were some 5,000 recorded lynchings in the United States. The rate reached a horrendous height around the beginning of the economic Depression in 1929.

A sharp and significant decrease in lynchings in this country, however, was around 1933 and 1934, during a period of acute capitalist economic crisis. Those years coincided with the rise of a mass workers' movement that organized African-American and white workers together into the CIO – the Congress of Industrial Organizations. It coincided with the rise of the 1934 general strikes of workers in San Francisco and Toledo and Minneapolis and military factory occupations – known as sit-down strikes – that swept from auto workers, to electric storage battery makers, to hosiery workers.

This ascending workers' movement did not put an end once and for all to lynchings. But it pushed back this and other forms of terror. And the degree to which right-wing violence has surged or been suppressed since then has depended on the relative strength of the working class in its struggle against the wealthy owning class. When the majority of working people awaken to their own class interests and act together to take collective action, the social equation is dramatically changed in a period of such rising struggle.

Many movements have come before the trans liberation movement: the movement to abolish slavery, women's suffrage, workers' rights, civil rights, gay liberation, anti-Vietnam war, women's liberation, Deaf and disabled liberation. These social movements have had a profound social impact on U.S. life.

Does our trans movement have to start from scratch or can we build on what we've learned from the last 150 years? What lessons can we glean from struggles that preceded ours? What are the best tactics and strategy to win our demands? How can we not only protect our victories, but gain new ground?

And where is the mass movement in the streets that trans liberation can ally itself with? Where is the struggle today that can turn the tide of reaction? Where are the hundreds of thousands in the streets, marching and demanding justice, like the protests of the 1930s that won the right to unionize, to Social Security, to welfare and unemployment insurance, to public housing? Today, Corporate America and its politicians are taking the reforms of the New Deal off the table. Where is the massive, angry response?

Is a mass upsurge possible today? If so, can we make the demands of the trans communities a strong voice within that tide of resistance? Who can we look toward to build such a movement?

All our lives we have been taught that those of us who do the work of the world are not the agents of historical change. Instead, we are told that the only way we can have any impact on the direction of the economy, or society as a whole, is to vote once every four years for one of two parties that are funded by and beholden to big business.

Since the 1930s, the Republican and Democratic Party have played hard cop, soft cop when it comes to domestic economic policy. The Democratic Party has taken credit for legislative reforms like the New Deal. But do the Democrats really deserve that credit? This is an important question, especially since some in the lesbian, gay, bi, and trans communities look to the Democratic Party as a vehicle of progressive reform. So how the New Deal was won, for example, has meaning for our movement.

Franklin Roosevelt, a Democrat, took office three years after the cataclysmic 1929 capitalist economic crash. His administration presided during a powerful mass upsurge of the working class that threatened to erupt into a general working-class rebellion. The Roosevelt administration was in charge of trying to quell this pre-revolutionary surge. His job was to save capitalism. And the New Deal was meant to do just that. And so the New Deal was a great legislative victory wrested through struggle. Workers won it.

Democrat Lyndon Johnson was similarly forced to make concessions as a result of the great struggles of the 1960s. His administration created new social programs like the "War on Poverty" in order to buy social peace at home, while waging war in Vietnam. These policies, plus the strong war economy, helped isolate young middle-class activists and keep rebellion from sweeping the entire working class.

The Democratic Party cannot lead us forward to trans liberation. They've led us into war and economic austerity: Woodrow Wilson led the United States into World War I; Franklin Roosevelt led the country into World War II. Truman started the Korean War. John Kennedy and Lyndon Johnson began and widened the Vietnam War.

The reactionary drive to slash social services began during the late 1970s, when Democrat Jimmy Carter started draining social services to fuel a $2 trillion military buildup. And he was the mastermind of the union-busting plan to attack the air traffic controllers – implemented by Reagan in 1981 – that was the opening gun of the current anti-labor offensive.

The process of transferring wealth from working people to the wealthy continued after Reagan. The rate actually accelerated during the first four years of the Clinton Democratic administration.

Whether a Democrat or a Republican presides, both parties administer the same system on behalf of big business. As the trans struggle unfolds, it will become critical to develop an independent movement that can free itself from the grip of "lesser-of-two-evils" politics of waiting to get another Democrat in office.

The truth is, you and I are the stuff that great leaders are made of. We don't have to wait for a distinguished white man on a horse or a politician wealthy enough to win office in a multimillion dollar campaign to usher in justice and equality. The ranks of rebellions and revolutions that have shaped human history have been made up of people like you and me. That history lesson has been purposefully kept from us.

Where is the great social movement in the streets that will help support and strengthen our demand for trans liberation? Will we see it in our lifetimes? No crystal ball exists to predict mass awakening. But laws of motion and development do exist: Repression breeds resistance. That's the lesson of Stonewall.

And remember what Sylvia Rivera said about that rebellion? "I always believed that we would have a fight back. I just didn't know it would be that night."

When I was growing up in the 1950s, the right-wing repression was ferocious. Working-class families like my own went about our lives, going to work, going to school, paying the bills, feeding the cat. We couldn't see the momentous struggles of the 1960s on the horizon. We didn't realize that the repression was making it impossible not to struggle, not to fight back.

Of all the periods of human history, I am excited to live in this particular epoch. In just five decades, I have witnessed technology outstrip anything I saw as a child in a Buck Rogers movie, or anything I read by Jules Vernes – Mars probes, Pentium chips, laser microsurgery. Yet sweatshop conditions today – in this country and around the world – are reminiscent of the nineteenth century exploitation of labor that I read about as a child in Charles Dickens's novels. It is this contradiction that creates the material basis for the inevitable rise of an independent, anti-capitalist movement by the working class.

Will trans people be in the front ranks of these battles? Of course we will be. Wherever oppression has existed, we have been at the forefront of struggles.

History has recorded the names of many trans warriors. We all grew up hearing about Joan of Arc, for example. Few of us, though, were taught that she was a masculine, cross-dressing female. Joan of Arc was an illiterate, peasant teenager. She became a brilliant leader of a peasant army because she was able to rise to the demands of the historical moment in which she lived.

So did the cross-dressed leaders of urban rebellions like "Captain" Alice Clark, a cross-dressed female who led a crowd of women and cross-dressed males in England in 1629 in an uprising over the high cost of grain. So did Rebecca and her Daughters — peasant guerrilla armies that shaped Welsh history by fighting British occupation in the nineteenth century. So did Louisa Capetillo, the Puerto Rican cross-dresser and socialist feminist who led tobacco workers in battles against their bosses in the early twentieth century. So did Magnus Hirschfeld, a Jewish, gay, feminine, socialist leader at the turn of the twentieth century who led a movement for the rights of trans people and same-sex love in Germany. So did Marsha Johnson and Sylvia Rivera, impoverished drag queens who fought the cops at the Stonewall Rebellion in 1969.

The irony is that many of those trans leaders did not fight only for civil rights for transgender, transsexual, intersexual, lesbian, gay, and bisexual people. They fought colonization, unjust wars, hunger, privatization of land, gouging taxation, repression by the police and military, homelessness, and economic exploitation. They fought for the rights of everyone who was tyrannized and downtrodden.

We remember their names for the same reason we remember Nat Turner's and Sojourner Truth's and John Brown's — because they fought back, even when the economic and social system that oppressed them seemed invincible. Imagine how during the nineteenth century in the United States it must have seemed as though slavery could last forever. There was no mass movement. They didn't have millions of followers. But Nat Turner, Sojourner Truth, and John Brown fought back anyway. In doing so, they became *catalysts* to the movement to abolish slavery.

The people who make a difference in history are those who fight for freedom — not because they're guaranteed to succeed — but because it's the right thing to do. And that's the kind of fighters that history demands today. Not those who worship the accomplished fact. Not those who can only believe in what is visible today. But instead, people of conscience who dedicate their lives to what needs to be won, and what can be won.

I am confident that you and I will find each other, shoulder-to-shoulder, in that historic struggle.

DEIRDRE SINNOTT (AL DENTE)

"*My goal is
to change society*"

Defining myself is hard; being myself is easy. Right now I describe myself as tri-gendered. Sometimes I look very masculine – I get called *sir* and *brother*. Other times I look more feminine and sometimes I try to look androgynous.

When people say to me "Thank you sir ... I mean ma'am ... I mean sir," I say "Don't worry. It's deliberate!" I've always had a deep voice and it helps with the illusion.

As far back as I can remember people have told me I look like a boy. I used to have what they called a pixie haircut. It wasn't my choice but everyone said what a cute boy I was. I told my mother that I wanted my hair long and that I would never wear anything but hip huggers and bell bottoms. She said, "never is a long time," and she was right.

I remember in sixth grade I wrote, "I want to be a boy," on the sidewalk with a piece of chalk. One of my friends asked me if I really meant it. I had just gone to a ballroom dance recital and worn stockings for the first time. I really liked the look and feel of the stockings. After thinking about it I said, "Well I guess not." I don't think I was totally committed to either gender as I understood them.

My gender expression goes in cycles, but no matter what I look like people call me *sir*. When I first heard the term *transgendered* I thought "Oh that's it. It fits." Other people recognized my gender difference long before I was ready to acknowledge it.

Most of my jobs over the years have been traditionally done by men. I've worked in the theater as electrician, carpenter, prop master, and stage manager. Now I'm a grassroots organizer and work designing Web pages. I never wanted to be thought of as vulnerable.

The other thing I am is a bisexual. I came out to my friends in high school in 1977. It caused a stir and some unnecessary hysteria, but for the most part my friends were supportive or curious. I have had lovers of both sexes and also of multiple genders.

Right now I'm happy with an eclectic collection of clothes so that I can decide each morning how I will present myself for the day. I know I'm oppressed because I'm a female who is differently gendered and a bisexual. This oppression affects the way I see things and the decisions I make. There are many places I don't feel are safe for someone like me. I've been threatened, spat at, and called names.

I've never wanted to change myself to conform to bigots. My goal is to change the society so that there isn't oppression. I've seen the difference the progressive movement can make in people's lives and how working collectively forges what might appear to be unlikely alliances. The struggle against racism, sexism, and queer-phobia is the best place to be. Human potential is vast and to tap into it we have to struggle.

DEIRDRE SINNOTT (DRAG NAME AL DENTE) WORKS WITH THE INTERNATIONAL ACTION CENTER AND THE NATIONAL PEOPLE'S CAMPAIGN IN NEW YORK CITY. IF YOU WANT TO GET INVOLVED WITH THESE ORGANIZATIONS, THEIR WEB ADDRESS IS: WWW.IACENTER.ORG.

Acknowledgments

I never would have lived to see the spring of 1997, let alone write this book, without the outpouring of love and support from friends, allies, activists, comrades, and other caring people throughout the United States and around the world. You helped my partner Minnie Bruce Pratt and me during my year of grave illness that ended in December 1996. I offer my heartfelt thanks to each of you for helping me tread water during that terrible time when I very nearly drowned.

This book includes adaptations of speeches I gave at conferences and rallies in the spring of 1997. I want to thank the organizers of those events. Those who deliver the keynotes or rev up the rallies from the podium receive high visibility. But as an organizer, I know just how much painstaking work went into building those events. Without the organizers there would be no podiums.

I am grateful to Gary Bowen, Cheryl Chase, Mike Hernandez, Craig Hickman, William Mason (Peaches), Linda Phillips, Cynthia Phillips, Sylvia Rivera, Deirdre Sinnott (Al Dente), and Dragon Xcalibur for contributing their truths, their insights, and their eloquence to this book – and to my life. Thank you Marilyn Humphries for the sensitivity of your vision behind the lens.

I thank my literary agent Charlotte Sheedy, my editor Amy Caldwell, the entire staff at Beacon Press, and my friend Deirdre Sinnott (Al Dente) for the work and confidence they put into this book.

And last, but not least, thank you Minnie Bruce Pratt – wife, partner, lover, friend, cothinker. You make even a day with catastrophic illness serenely exhilarating. *"Loving everything about you, I forget nothing."*